POVERTY

Opposing Viewpoints®

OTHER BOOKS OF RELATED INTEREST

POVERTY

Opposing Viewpoints®

David L. Bender, *Publisher*

Bruno Leone, *Executive Editor*

Bonnie Szumski, *Editorial Director*

Brenda Stalcup, *Managing Editor*

Scott Barbour, *Senior Editor*

Laura K. Egendorf, *Book Editor*

OPPOSING VIEWPOINTS® SERIES

Greenhaven Press, Inc., San Diego, California

Cover photo: Dave Allen

Library of Congress Cataloging-in-Publication Data

Poverty : opposing viewpoints / Laura K. Egendorf, book editor.
    p.   cm. — (Opposing viewpoints series)
  Includes bibliographical references and index.
  ISBN 1-56510-947-3 (lib. bdg. : alk. paper). —
ISBN 1-56510-946-5 (pbk. : alk. paper)
  1. Poor—United States. 2. Poverty—United States. 3. Public
welfare—United States. I. Egendorf, Laura K., 1973–   . II. Series:
Opposing viewpoints series (Unnumbered)
HV91.P694 1999
362.5'0973—dc21   98-17866
                                                                        CIP

Greenhaven Press, Inc., P.O. Box 289009
San Diego, CA 92198-9009

"CONGRESS SHALL MAKE NO LAW...ABRIDGING THE FREEDOM OF SPEECH, OR OF THE PRESS."

First Amendment to the U.S. Constitution

The basic foundation of our democracy is the First Amendment guarantee of freedom of expression. The Opposing Viewpoints Series is dedicated to the concept of this basic freedom and the idea that it is more important to practice it than to enshrine it.

CONTENTS

WHY CONSIDER
OPPOSING VIEWPOINTS?

"The only way in which a human being can make some approach to knowing the whole of a subject is by hearing what can be said about it by persons of every variety of opinion and studying all modes in which it can be looked at by every character of mind. No wise man ever acquired his wisdom in any mode but this."

John Stuart Mill

In our media-intensive culture it is not difficult to find differing opinions. Thousands of newspapers and magazines and dozens of radio and television talk shows resound with differing points of view. The difficulty lies in deciding which opinion to agree with and which "experts" seem the most credible. The more inundated we become with differing opinions and claims, the more essential it is to hone critical reading and thinking skills to evaluate these ideas. Opposing Viewpoints books address this problem directly by presenting stimulating debates that can be used to enhance and teach these skills. The varied opinions contained in each book examine many different aspects of a single issue. While examining these conveniently edited opposing views, readers can develop critical thinking skills such as the ability to compare and contrast authors' credibility, facts, argumentation styles, use of persuasive techniques, and other stylistic tools. In short, the Opposing Viewpoints Series is an ideal way to attain the higher-level thinking and reading skills so essential in a culture of diverse and contradictory opinions.

In addition to providing a tool for critical thinking, Opposing Viewpoints books challenge readers to question their own strongly held opinions and assumptions. Most people form their opinions on the basis of upbringing, peer pressure, and personal, cultural, or professional bias. By reading carefully balanced opposing views, readers must directly confront new ideas as well as the opinions of those with whom they disagree. This is not to simplistically argue that everyone who reads opposing views will—or should—change his or her opinion. Instead, the series enhances readers' understanding of their own views by encouraging confrontation with opposing ideas. Careful examination of others' views can lead to the readers' understanding of the logical inconsistencies in their own opinions, perspective on why they hold an opinion, and the consideration of the possibility that their opinion requires further evaluation.

EVALUATING OTHER OPINIONS

To ensure that this type of examination occurs, Opposing Viewpoints books present all types of opinions. Prominent spokespeople on different sides of each issue as well as well-known professionals from many disciplines challenge the reader. An additional goal of the series is to provide a forum for other, less known, or even unpopular viewpoints. The opinion of an ordinary person who has had to make the decision to cut off life support from a terminally ill relative, for example, may be just as valuable and provide just as much insight as a medical ethicist's professional opinion. The editors have two additional purposes in including these less known views. One, the editors encourage readers to respect others' opinions—even when not enhanced by professional credibility. It is only by reading or listening to and objectively evaluating others' ideas that one can determine whether they are worthy of consideration. Two, the inclusion of such viewpoints encourages the important critical thinking skill of objectively evaluating an author's credentials and bias. This evaluation will illuminate an author's reasons for taking a particular stance on an issue and will aid in readers' evaluation of the author's ideas.

As series editors of the Opposing Viewpoints Series, it is our hope that these books will give readers a deeper understanding of the issues debated and an appreciation of the complexity of even seemingly simple issues when good and honest people disagree. This awareness is particularly important in a democratic society such as ours in which people enter into public debate to determine the common good. Those with whom one disagrees should not be regarded as enemies but rather as people whose views deserve careful examination and may shed light on one's own.

Thomas Jefferson once said that "difference of opinion leads to inquiry, and inquiry to truth." Jefferson, a broadly educated man, argued that "if a nation expects to be ignorant and free . . . it expects what never was and never will be." As individuals and as a nation, it is imperative that we consider the opinions of others and examine them with skill and discernment. The Opposing Viewpoints Series is intended to help readers achieve this goal.

David L. Bender & Bruno Leone,
Series Editors

Greenhaven Press anthologies primarily consist of previously published material taken from a variety of sources, including periodicals, books, scholarly journals, newspapers, government documents, and position papers from private and public organizations. These original sources are often edited for length and to ensure their accessibility for a young adult audience. The anthology editors also change the original titles of these works in order to clearly present the main thesis of each viewpoint and to explicitly indicate the opinion presented in the viewpoint. These alterations are made in consideration of both the reading and comprehension levels of a young adult audience. Every effort is made to ensure that Greenhaven Press accurately reflects the original intent of the authors included in this anthology.

INTRODUCTION

"On the basis of consumption, Americans are far more equal than income alone would suggest."

—Bruce Bartlett

"If the United States is truly concerned about poverty and its consequences, we must be aware of the real extent of economic deprivation in this society."

—Ruth Sidel

There is no one-size-fits-all definition of poverty. The poorest people in an industrialized nation may well be richer than the average citizen of a less-developed country. According to the *United Nations' Human Development Report 1996*, the average per capita income of the poorest one-fifth of Americans was $5,814 in 1993. That figure is ten times Tanzania's average per capita income of $580 per year. By Tanzanian standards, Americans in that bottom 20 percent may seem quite well-off. However, by U.S. standards, they are not.

Politicians and social scientists have sought to define poverty for over three decades. In 1965, the government officially adopted the definition set by Mollie Orshansky of the Social Security Administration, who placed the poverty threshold at an income three times the cost of a minimally nutritious diet. The threshold for a family of four in 1996 was $16,036. Similarly, the poverty guidelines established by the U.S. Department of Health and Human Services (HHS) placed the poverty level for a family of four at $16,450 in 1998. (Since 1966, poverty guidelines have been set higher in Alaska and Hawaii.) The poverty rate in 1996, according to the HHS, was 13.7 percent, or 36.5 million Americans.

Although these figures may seem straightforward, experts disagree as to whether they are the most accurate measurements of poverty. Some believe poverty is overestimated, while others claim it is underestimated. Those who say poverty is overestimated argue that certain income sources—including unreported wages and government entitlements such as food stamps, Medicaid, and public housing—are not taken into account when a family's annual income is measured. Critics also contend that the cost of living is overstated, further skewing the poverty rate. According to Lowell Gallaway, a professor of economics at Ohio

University, the poverty rate is overstated by a factor of two.

Additionally, conservatives maintain, most poor Americans do not live substandard lives, further indicating that poverty is not as extensive as the official figures would indicate. They point out that most poor American families own more luxury items and consumer appliances than average Europeans do. According to *Human Development Report*, the average per capita income in the Netherlands is $17,330, approximately three times larger than the per capita income of the poorest one-fifth in the United States. However, in 1994, nearly 93 percent of poor American families had a color television, almost 72 percent had at least one car, and approximately 60 percent had a microwave and a VCR. In comparison, in 1991 only 50 percent of all households in the Netherlands had a VCR and just 22 percent owned a microwave. Hence, as Bruce Bartlett writes, "Insofar as consumption is a truer measure of living standards than income, . . . many low-income Americans are far better off than their reported income suggests."

On the other hand, liberal analysts claim that the rate of poverty is underestimated. For example, they contend, the current method of measuring income based on pre-tax earnings is deceptive. When income is based on after-tax earnings, the poverty rate climbs to over 23 percent. These analysts also assert that the current definition of poverty does not take into account the true costs of living. According to political scientists John Schwarz and Thomas Volgy, the average family now spends only one-sixth of its income on food. The costs of housing, child care, transportation, and health care are not taken into consideration, these critics contend. The poverty guideline for a family of three—for example, a mother with two children—is $13,650 per year. However, women's advocates argue that mothers on welfare in California would need to earn two to three times the minimum wage—or an annual salary between $25,000 and $35,000—in order to provide their family with housing and other key expenses.

The costs of housing are especially important when determining the true extent of poverty, some advocates for the poor contend. These advocates point out that housing—an essential—is the largest portion of many poor families' budgets. Shirley Weathers, the author of a report published by the Utah Issues Information Program, argues that housing expenses, rather than food expenses, provide a more realistic measure of income inadequacy. Weathers notes that poor families are often left with inadequate funds to pay bills or purchase food and clothing after paying their housing costs. "On the average in the 1960s housing costs represented one-quarter of a family's budget whereas shelter is now more likely to constitute one-half of the living costs of a low-income family," she writes.

Some of these arguments, such as including noncash benefits and basing income on after-tax earnings, have been taken into consideration by the U.S. Census Bureau. In September 1997, Daniel H. Weinberg, the chief of Housing and Household for the Economic Statistics Division of the U.S. Census Bureau, reported that the bureau has computed seventeen experimental definitions of income to determine the effect of noncash benefits and taxes. If noncash benefits are included and taxes are subtracted, the estimated poverty rate would be 10.2 percent, or 27.1 million Americans, according to the bureau. The Census Bureau is examining recommendations to change the official definition of poverty. As of this writing, no decision has been made. If this decision were left to the American public, it is likely that the poverty rate would increase: Polls have indicated that most Americans believe the poverty threshold should be adjusted upward by 25 percent.

Whether the official definition of poverty will be adjusted remains to be seen. As it stands, the debate over defining poverty centers on whether poverty should be determined by consumption or expenditure—that is, do poor people have more spending power than their official income indicates, or are their essential expenses not fully taken into account? *Poverty: Opposing Viewpoints* considers these and other related questions in the following chapters: Is Poverty a Serious Problem? What Are the Causes of Poverty? Can People Work Their Way out of Poverty? How Can Poor People Be Helped? In these chapters, the authors debate the extent and causes of poverty in America and possible measures to help the poor.

CHAPTER 1

IS POVERTY A SERIOUS PROBLEM?

CHAPTER PREFACE

One measure of the severity of poverty is the quantity and quality of an impoverished person's diet. Although few people would argue that hunger in America is at the level of a country such as North Korea or Somalia, there is debate over whether or not hunger is a serious problem in the United States.

Some people argue that hunger in the United States is a serious problem, especially for poor children. In January 1998, *Christian Social Action* magazine reported that over 34 million Americans are threatened by food insecurity, defined by the U.S. Department of Agriculture as "limited or uncertain availability of nutritionally adequate foods." Of these Americans, 11.2 million experience food insecurity accompanied by moderate or severe hunger. A 1994 study by the Food Research and Action Center concluded that 5 million American children under the age of twelve go hungry each month. The homeless and unemployed are not the only ones who experience hunger, some observers contend. The working poor are becoming a more common sight at food pantries and soup kitchens, according to advocates for the poor.

Other commentators reject the argument that hunger is pervasive in America. Robert Rector, a poverty analyst for the Heritage Foundation, a conservative think tank, notes that poor children in America consume 211 percent of the recommended daily allowance for protein. Rector comments, "The U.S. Department of Health and Human Services reports that the top nutrition-related health problem facing poor Americans is now obesity." Another study indicates that in 1990, the poor spent a smaller percentage of their resources on food than in 1970. Some economists believe that spending a decreased proportion of overall resources on food is a sign of improved living standards.

Hunger is just one of the yardsticks—along with income level and the economic condition of the working poor—for measuring poverty. In the following chapter, the authors debate whether poverty is a serious problem in the United States.

| "Federal and state antipoverty programs have lifted millions of children and disabled and elderly people out of poverty."

GOVERNMENT PROGRAMS HAVE REDUCED POVERTY

Bob Herbert

Government antipoverty programs have made poverty a less serious problem in the United States, argues Bob Herbert in the following viewpoint. According to Herbert, children and the elderly have benefited greatly from safety net programs. He asserts that the welfare bill signed by President Bill Clinton in August 1996, which cut many of the benefits provided by these programs, will increase poverty. Herbert is a syndicated columnist.

As you read, consider the following questions:

1. What would the poverty rate among the elderly have been in 1995 if safety net programs had not been in place, according to the study cited by the author?
2. According to Herbert, how did government poverty policy differ during the recessions of the early 1980s and early 1990s?

A gain and again during the fight over welfare we heard self-righteous, sanctimonious and often very rich politicians proclaim that anti-poverty programs hadn't worked. The programs were actually harming the poor, they said. Echoing Charles Dickens' most unforgiving villains, they reasoned that the best approach would be to cut the poor's already meager benefits. That would build character, they said. So they cut the benefits and called it reform.

In a December 1996 radio address, President Bill Clinton reaffirmed his solidarity with those who believe that removing a plate of spaghetti or a bowl of rice and beans from the dinner table of a hungry child is somehow beneficial.

From his wobbly perch atop the tower of national virtue, the president spoke of his "moral obligation" to help the poor help themselves.

"The door has now been opened to a new era of freedom and independence," Clinton said, an apparent reference to the sense of liberation that the well-off have always associated with bare cupboards and eviction notices. He might also have mentioned the unparalleled exhilaration that comes from an empty stomach.

In any event, the message of the president and others is quite clear: It is time to take the scissors to the safety net.

From another quarter—less cynical, more compassionate, more in touch with the real world—comes a study that shows how important government programs continue to be in helping Americans, young and old, escape the dangerous and demoralizing grasp of poverty.

GOVERNMENT PROGRAMS WORK

The study was done by the Center on Budget and Policy Priorities and its findings are not ambiguous: "Based on analysis of recently released Census Bureau data, this paper shows that federal and state antipoverty programs have lifted millions of children and disabled and elderly people out of poverty. Many of those who remained poor were significantly less poor than they would have been without government assistance."

The study found that without such assistance, 57.6 million people would have been poor in 1995. "But when government benefits are counted, including food stamps, housing assistance, school lunch support and benefits provided through the earned-income tax credit, the number of poor people drops to 30.3 million."

Safety net programs, especially Social Security, held the

poverty rate among the elderly in 1995 to 9 percent. Without them, according to the study, the poverty rate among the elderly would have been 50 percent.

WELFARE REFORM WILL HURT CHILDREN

In early September 1995, liberal Senator Daniel Patrick Moynihan asked his colleagues to picture in their minds what conditions for poor children would be like in ten years if the proposed "welfare-reform" measure passed. He then painted a scenario of people picking up on winter mornings the frozen bodies of youngsters who had fallen asleep on street grates. Shortly afterward, conservative columnist George Will sounded a similar note of disgust in the *Washington Post* regarding the pending bill: "No child is going to be spiritually improved by being collateral damage in a bombardment of severities targeted at adults who may or may not deserve more severe treatment from the welfare system."

Thomas J. Osborne, *Humanist*, January/February 1997.

Among children, means-tested programs, including Aid to Families with Dependent Children, have the biggest effect. The study said: "The safety net programs reduced the child poverty rate from 24 percent before benefits are counted to 16 percent."

You would think such substantial bulwarks against poverty would be widely applauded. Instead, anti-poverty efforts in general are derided and the mere mention of welfare makes many Americans apoplectic.

POVERTY IN RECESSIONS

The lead author of the study, entitled "The Safety Net Delivers," was Wendell Primus, a former assistant secretary of health and human services who left the Clinton administration in protest in the summer of 1996 when the president signed a welfare bill that will result in an estimated one million children being thrown into poverty.

Primus and his co-authors took a close look at two periods of recent history: the early 1980s, when government anti-poverty benefits were substantially reduced, and the mid-80s to mid-90s, when bipartisan efforts to increase government assistance and expand the earned-income tax credit strengthened the safety net.

Recessions occurred during both periods. The study found that when government benefits are taken into account, "The number of people who were poor grew by 11 million during the recession of the early 1980s and by only 5.5 million—just half as much—during the recession of the early 1990s. Poverty grew far less during the most recent recession because the safety net was considerably stronger in the early-1990s."

In other words, the programs worked.

But we now have, for the poor, the toxic combination of Bill Clinton in the White House and the Republican Party in control of both houses of Congress. The next recession will provide tremendous opportunities for character-building.

> "The current system has not
> resolved—rather seems to be
> perpetuating—poverty."

GOVERNMENT ANTIPOVERTY PROGRAMS WORSEN POVERTY

Dick Armey

In the following viewpoint, Dick Armey asserts that government antipoverty programs actually create greater material poverty. Armey, a Republican congressman from Texas, claims that an increase in welfare benefits leads to a decrease in the earned income of the recipients. In addition, he maintains, children of welfare recipients are more likely than other children to need welfare as adults, further indicating the failure of the welfare system. For those reasons, Armey argues, welfare reform is necessary. In 1996, two years after the publication of this viewpoint, Congress passed a welfare reform bill that set lifetime limits on benefits and restricted benefits for immigrants, teenage parents, and childless adults.

As you read, consider the following questions:

1. According to Armey, how does welfare penalize marriage?
2. What percentage of the children born in 1980 will live on welfare, in the author's view?
3. According to the author, by what percentage does welfare reduce the probability of a person or family escaping poverty in a particular year?

Reprinted from Dick Armey, "Public Welfare in America," *Journal of Social, Political, and Economic Studies*, Summer 1994, by permission.

When President Lyndon Johnson launched his Unconditional War on Poverty, he boldly declared, "the days of the dole in the United States country are numbered." However, within two years of the enactment of his Economic Opportunity Act of 1964, a remarkable escalation in public assistance payments began. While President Johnson may have been correct that the days of welfare are numbered, that number is proving to be very large indeed.

PERPETUATING POVERTY

Any attempt to reform welfare must begin with the recognition that the current system has not resolved—rather seems to be perpetuating—poverty. It has created behavioral disincentives that trap many recipients in poverty from generation to generation and has also created yet another unwieldy and unresponsive bureaucracy. The key dilemma of the welfare state is that prolific spending intended to alleviate material poverty has caused the collapse of the low-income family and led to a dramatic increase in behavioral poverty—dependency, lack of educational aspiration and achievement, increased single parenthood and illegitimacy.

Studies have consistently shown that higher welfare benefits decrease work effort and increase welfare dependence. Increased dependence, in turn, has strong negative effects on children's intellectual abilities and life prospects. . . .

Although the poverty rate has remained relatively steady since 1965, welfare spending has risen from 1.5 percent of gross national product (GNP) when Lyndon Johnson launched the program in 1965 to 5 percent today. The federal government spends more than $240 billion on welfare annually, which is more than twice the money needed to raise every person on welfare out of poverty.

NO INCENTIVES TO MARRY

It is no longer a question of whether this money has produced positive results, but rather what can be done to erase the debilitating effects welfare has had on society.

The system has made marriage economically irrational for most low-income parents. Welfare has converted the low-income working husband from a necessary breadwinner into a financial handicap. It has transformed marriage from a legal institution that protects and nurtures children into an institution that financially penalizes nearly all low-income parents who choose it. Welfare benefits will be higher if a man and woman do not marry and are treated by the government as separate "households."

Too many mothers decide not to marry the fathers of their children; they marry welfare instead. As George Gilder, author of *Wealth and Poverty* observed, the modern welfare state has convinced poor fathers that they are dispensable. . . .

THE DEMOGRAPHICS OF POVERTY

The poverty rate among those living in traditional married couple families is less than half the overall poverty rate; the poverty rate for female headed families (with no husband present) is nearly six times the poverty rate for traditional two parent families. Individuals living alone outside a family similarly have very high poverty rates.

According to U.S. Census Bureau data, 64 percent of welfare recipients are white, 31 percent are black, 14 percent are Hispanic and five percent are classified as "other." 42 percent of recipients are under 18, 48 percent are between the ages of 18 and 64, 10 percent are over 65. 48 percent of recipients have less than four years of high school education, 33 percent are high school graduates, and 18 percent have had at least one year of college. 57 percent of recipients are female, 43 percent are male.

More than 20 percent of the children born in the late 1960s have spent at least one year on welfare; more than 70 percent of black children born in the same period have done so. More than 30 percent of all children born in 1980 will live on welfare, as will 80 percent of black children. A majority (over 54 percent) of persons receiving means-tested income transfers in 1990 were *not* in poverty, as it is officially defined.

WELFARE'S CULTURE OF DEPENDENCY

Children raised in families that receive welfare assistance are themselves three times more likely than other children to be on welfare when they become adults. This inter-generational dependency is a clear indication that the welfare system is failing in its effort to lift people from poverty to self-sufficiency. A recent study found that higher welfare benefits increased the number of women who left the labor force and enrolled in welfare. A 50 percent increase in monthly Aid to Families with Dependent Children (AFDC) and Food Stamp benefit levels led to a 75 percent increase in both the number of women enrolling in AFDC and in the number of years spent on AFDC. The percentage of children receiving AFDC is higher in states with the highest AFDC payments and lower in states with the lowest AFDC payments.

The Office of Economic Opportunity conducted controlled experiments between 1971 and 1978 in Seattle and Denver, known as the Seattle/Denver Income Maintenance Experiment (SIME/DIME). The experiments found that increasing welfare benefits had a dramatic negative effect on labor force participation and earnings. For every $100 of extra welfare given to low-income persons, the earned income of the recipients fell by $80. Welfare reduces the probability that a poor person or family will leave poverty in any given year by about 60 percent. The chances of rising above the poverty level are two and one-half times greater if an individual or family does not receive welfare. At any one time, more than half of welfare recipients have been on welfare for ten years.

"I don't want to frighten you, but mean spirited Republicans are actually trying to tear this place down and put you out in the...gasp...real world!"

Reprinted by permission of Ed Gamble.

When the Great Society was launched in 1965, the illegitimacy rate among blacks was 25 percent; today, it is 66 percent. If current trends continue, the black illegitimate birth rate will reach 75 percent in ten years. Thirty years ago, one in every 40 white children was born to an unmarried mother; today, it is one in five.

The current system's financial penalties on marriage can be correlated with an unprecedented and growing number of unwed mother welfare recipients. The percentage of welfare recipients living in female-headed households increased from 29 percent in 1964 to 61 percent in 1976.

The Impact of Single Parent Families

White women raised in single parent homes are 164 percent more likely to bear children out of wedlock themselves and 111 percent more likely to have children as teenagers. Of those who do marry, marriages are 92 percent more likely to end in divorce than are the marriages of women raised in two parent families. Similar trends are also found among black women.

Children raised in single parent families, when compared to those in intact families, are one-third more likely to exhibit behavioral problems such as hyperactivity, antisocial behavior, and anxiety. Children in single parent families are two to three times more likely to need psychiatric care than those in two parent families; they are also more likely to commit suicide as teenagers. Children in single parent families score lower on IQ, aptitude and achievement tests. With family income, neighborhood, parental education, and other variables held constant, young black men from single parent homes are twice as likely to commit crimes and end up in jail than are similar young men in low-income families where the father is present.

The Failure of Welfare Reform

Welfare rolls have increased sharply since the 1988 welfare reform legislation became law. Less than one percent of the welfare population is working today. And the program has cost us $10 billion more than expected—$13 billion instead of $3 billion. At the time of enactment, it was predicted that the number of families on AFDC would not reach five million until late 1998. In fact, that milestone was reached in early 1993.

While Americans were told that the 1988 reforms required most welfare recipients to work for benefits, by 1992 only one percent of all AFDC parents was actually required to enroll in workfare in exchange for welfare benefits.

Welfare reform must begin with the realization that most programs designed to alleviate "material poverty" generally lead to an increase in "behavioral" poverty. While the poor were supposed to be the beneficiaries of the War on Poverty, they instead have become its victims.

| "Major antipoverty programs . . .
were meant to provide benefits that
reduce misery—and they have."

THE CONDITION OF THE POOR IS IMPROVING

Part I: Susan Mayer and Christopher Jencks,
Part II: *American Enterprise*

In Part I of the following two-part viewpoint, Susan Mayer and
Christopher Jencks contend that successful government programs
such as Medicaid, food stamps, and low-income housing subsidies have improved the health and welfare of poor families. In Part
II, the editors of the *American Enterprise* argue that the prevalence of
poverty in America has been exaggerated because of an apparent
overstatement of the cost of living as measured by the Consumer
Price Index. The editors maintain that contrary to discouraging
statistics, the quality of life has improved in America. Mayer is a
professor of public policy at the University of Chicago. Jencks is a
professor of public policy at the Kennedy School of Government
at Harvard University in Cambridge, Massachusetts. *American Enterprise* is a bimonthly magazine of politics, business, and culture.

As you read, consider the following questions:

1. According to Mayer and Jencks, how have the housing
   conditions of the poor improved?
2. What was the poverty rate among the elderly in 1992,
   according to Mayer and Jencks?
3. According to the editors of *American Enterprise*, what is the
   accurate number of Americans in poverty, based on price
   index adjustments?

Part I: Reprinted from Susan E. Mayer and Christopher Jencks, "War on Poverty: No
Apologies, Please," *The New York Times*, November 9, 1995, ©1995 by The New York Times
Company. Reprinted by permission. Part II: Reprinted by permission from "Blue-Ribbon
Commission Suggests Poverty in America Is Over-estimated," *The American Enterprise*,
January/February 1996, reprinted by permission of *The American Enterprise*, a Washington-
based magazine of politics, business, and culture.

I

As the White House and Congress struggle over the future shape of American government, one of the Republicans' most frequent arguments for cutting social programs is that they don't work.

ANTIPOVERTY PROGRAMS WORK

Millions of Americans, including a majority of legislators, seem to believe this claim. Yet almost all the evidence suggests that it is false. Most of the big antipoverty programs have done what they were meant to do. Anyone who bothers to look at the Federal Government's surveys of how Americans have lived over the last generation can see this. But hardly anyone looks.

Federal, state and local governments spent about $300 billion on programs for the poor in 1993. The six biggest programs were Medicaid ($132 billion), food stamps ($26 billion), Supplemental Security Income ($26 billion), Aid to Families With Dependent Children ($25 billion), low-income housing subsidies ($20 billion) and Head Start and other compensatory education ($10 billion). Medicaid, food stamps, housing subsidies and S.S.I. clearly did what they were meant to do. A.F.D.C. and compensatory education programs have had mixed records, but neither is a clear failure.

Medicaid was established in 1965 to improve poor people's access to medical care. Before 1965, the Federal Government's annual Health Interview Survey showed that the lowest income group typically made 20 percent fewer doctor visits a year than the highest income group. This was true despite the fact that poor people were more likely to suffer from almost every kind of sickness. By 1980, however, income no longer had any detectable effect on the odds that someone who was sick would consult a doctor.

Food stamps became a national program in 1970. Five years earlier, the National Food Consumption Survey had found that poor families ate substantially less than others. The next such survey, in 1977, found that the effects of family income on food consumption had been cut in half. Hunger and malnutrition were also much harder to find.

HOUSING AND EDUCATION PROGRAMS

Many Americans see government housing programs for the poor as a failure, because they assume that the money goes into huge high-rise projects that foster crime and social ills. Concentrating the poor in a few high-rises was a mistake. But we haven't built such projects for a generation. Since 1975, almost all Federal money for low-income housing has gone to help poor families pay their rent in private apartments.

Conditions in these units are quite good. The Census Bureau's housing survey shows that nearly every measure of poor families' housing conditions has improved since the early 1970s. The poor are less likely to have holes in their floors, cracks in their walls or ceilings, and leaky roofs. They are more likely to have complete plumbing, central heat and electrical outlets in every room.

The war on poverty also included two relatively small compensatory education programs—Head Start for preschoolers and Chapter 1 for elementary school children—to improve poor children's achievement. Most evaluations show that children who are enrolled in these programs learn somewhat more than comparable children who are not. But once these programs end, their benefits appear to fade. They are not a permanent vaccine against the costs of living in the wrong family or attending the wrong schools.

If we really want to know whether compensatory education has long-term benefits, we must ask whether those who have received more of it know more when they finish school than similar students who got less or none. We have no studies of this kind. The National Assessment of Educational Progress shows, however, that the proportion of 17-year-olds with very low reading and math scores has fallen substantially since the early 1970s. This suggests that the cumulative effect of compensatory education and other changes may have been significant at the bottom of the income scale.

AIDING THE ELDERLY AND CHILDREN

The United States also has two big programs that give cash to poor people. Supplemental Security Income, created in 1972, provides a minimum monthly income for the elderly and disabled. Congress also made Social Security benefits for the elderly and disabled far more generous after 1972. If S.S.I. and improvements in Social Security had done what they were meant to do, poverty among the elderly should have dropped after 1972. It did. The official poverty rate among the elderly fell from 19 percent in 1972 to 15 percent in 1982 to 12 percent in 1992. Here again, Government spending worked.

The most controversial antipoverty program is Aid to Families With Dependent Children. A.F.D.C. was created in 1935, when most single mothers were widows and nobody wanted them to work. The program was already unpopular when President Lyndon Johnson declared war on poverty in 1964, so he did nothing to expand it. States have always set A.F.D.C. benefits well below the poverty line, so welfare has never done much to reduce the official poverty count. It survived only because it was the cheapest plan anyone could devise for keeping poor children with their mother when their father was not around and for keeping a roof over the family's head. That is still true today. [The 1996 welfare reform bill replaced A.F.D.C. with Temporary Assistance to Needy Families (TANF).]

THE LIVING STANDARDS OF THE POOR

• In 1991 nearly 40 percent of all "poor" households owned their own homes.

• Nearly 60 percent of poor households have more than two rooms per person. Nearly 60 percent have air conditioning.

• Sixty-four percent of "poor" households own a car; 14 percent own two or more cars.

• Fifty-six percent own microwave ovens. Around a quarter have an automatic dishwasher; nearly one-third own a separate, stand-alone freezer.

• Ninety-one percent have a color television; 29 percent own two or more.

Robert Rector, *American Enterprise*, January/February 1995.

Conservatives often cite increases in the welfare rolls as evidence that the war on poverty failed, but their statistics are very selective. The A.F.D.C. rolls grew between 1965 and 1975 partly because the number of single mothers grew and partly because Federal court decisions and changes in state regulations made it easier for single mothers to get benefits. Since 1975 the rolls have grown at about the same rate as the total population. In 1993, for example, 13 percent of all children received A.F.D.C., compared with 11 percent in 1983 and 12 percent in 1975.

America's official poverty rate is based solely on people's cash income. Except for S.S.I., major antipoverty programs have all had one thing in common: they never tried to raise anyone's income above the poverty line. They were meant to provide benefits that reduce misery—and they have.

NO EFFECT ON BIRTH RATES

Those who claim we lost the war on poverty point to increases in teenage childbearing, unwed parenthood and violent crime. But if these problems are linked to antipoverty spending, the relationship is hard to detect. The birth rate among teenagers fell by a quarter between 1964 and 1980, when antipoverty spending was rising faster. It rose in the late 1980s and early 1990s, when real A.F.D.C. benefits fell.

It is true that prospective parents of all ages were less likely to marry in 1980 than in 1964, and that A.F.D.C. benefits also rose in those years. But unwed parenthood continued to increase after 1980, when the value of the welfare package began to decline. Violent crime also increased between 1964 and 1974, but the National Criminal Victimization Survey shows no consistent trend since then.

So when we look at the overall antipoverty effort, the bottom line looks quite good. Medicaid, food stamps, rent subsidies and S.S.I. all did what they were meant to do. The value of compensatory education is still uncertain. One program, A.F.D.C., was always politically unpopular but survived because it was cheaper than any politically acceptable alternative. This is not a record for which liberal politicians need apologize. Nor is it evidence that government spending does not work.

II

In 1995, a commission of economists headed by Stanford University's Michael Boskin met to study the way government agencies measure inflation via the so-called Consumer Price Index, or CPI. One reason that subject is important to more than just statisticians is because the CPI is used to adjust the nation's income and poverty numbers. If inflation is being mismeasured every year, then income and poverty will be too. Over a period of years, our understanding of how our quality of life is progressing can be badly skewed.

In addition to Boskin, former chairman of the president's Council of Economic Advisers and an adjunct scholar at the American Enterprise Institute, the blue ribbon commission included eminent scholars like Dale Jorgenson, an expert on measuring economic growth and former winner of the John Bates Clark award for best American economist under age 40, and Zvi Griliches of Harvard, former president of the American Economic Association and an authority on the measurement of quality changes in goods and services. The group issued their report in September 1995.

AN OVERSTATED PRICE INDEX

For purposes of understanding U.S. income trends and poverty, the most important finding of the Boskin Commission was that the CPI has overstated the rise in the cost of living in recent years by about 1.5 percent a year. That may not sound like much to a layman, but it's a very big deal. Economics writer Jonathan Marshall illustrates why:

> Say your boss gave you a 3 percent raise last year, but prices rose 2½ percent, according to the government. That left you thinking you came away with only half a percent more purchasing power after inflation. . . . Now say the government got its figures wrong and prices really climbed only 1.5 percent. In that case your buying power actually rose 1.5 percent—three times as much as you originally thought. Over a decade, that difference would compound into sizable sums.

If the Boskin Commission economists are right, median weekly earnings for full-time male workers didn't *fall* 12 percent from 1979 to 1994, as the gloomy official numbers suggest— they actually *rose* 14 percent. And women's earnings over the same period didn't rise 7 percent as published, but actually zoomed upward 35 percent.

IMPROVEMENTS IN WELL-BEING

The number of Americans in poverty under these revised figures is enormously different than officially advertised. If the CPI has been overstated by 1.5 percent a year since 1967, there are 15 million poor instead of 38 million.

Marshall comments:

> These revisions to the wage and poverty picture may seem fancifully rosy, but they fit with other facts about improvements in people's material well-being. From 1970 to 1990, Americans' life expectancy rose to 75 years from 71 years. The share of households without a telephone fell to 5 percent from 13 percent. The share of households with color TVs soared to 96 percent from 34 percent. The number of households with cable TV jumped to 55 million from 4 million.

The Boskin Commission spelled out a variety of reasons why the CPI seems to be overstating the cost of living. These include:

> Overlooking consumer substitutions of cheaper goods for more pricey ones, like the shift from beef to chicken.

> Missing improvements in quality and efficiency in new goods which mean that consumers are getting much more for the same dollar spent—as when they get a bigger refrigerator that runs on less energy for the same amount an inferior fridge cost a decade earlier.

> Failing to take account of the mass switchover of consumers from shopping at department stores and regular groceries to dis-

count outlets instead, where they get the same goods for less than official retail prices.

Leaving out new products and services that improve human welfare.

"Just momentous" is how Harvard economist Jorgenson summarized the commission's findings to Marshall. "This," he notes, "could revolutionize the whole standard-of-living story."

"Not only are certain groups
particularly hard hit by poverty, but
poverty is often spatially
concentrated as well."

THE CONDITION OF THE POOR IS WORSENING

Marie Kennedy

In the following viewpoint, Marie Kennedy asserts that poverty
and income inequality have increased in recent years to the extent that ghetto neighborhoods share the characteristics of former colonies in the Third World. According to Kennedy, 11 million children suffer from hunger or substantial food shortages,
and the availability of public housing units has been sharply reduced. She argues that the poor are becoming marginalized in
society, thereby worsening their condition. This marginalization
is evident in the use of the term "underclass" and in the belief
of policy makers that poverty is caused by pathological behaviors, she contends. Kennedy is a professor of community planning at the University of Massachusetts in Boston. She also
works with Roofless Women's Action Research Mobilization, a
research and activist project that focuses on the problem of
homelessness among women.

As you read, consider the following questions:

1. What percentage of single female-headed families were in
   poverty in 1992, according to the author?
2. In Kennedy's view, what happened to government-subsidized
   housing in the 1980s and 1990s?
3. According to Kennedy, what should be the main resource in
   solving poverty?

Reprinted from Marie Kennedy, "The Poverty Epidemic," *Crossroads*, April 1995, by
permission.

As the right-wing rhetoric of Newt Gingrich and company increasingly dehumanizes and demonizes the poor in the U.S., the reality of poor people's lives and the voices of poor people themselves figure less and less in the public debate. Adding to the tendency for the middle class (and even some of the poor themselves) to see large sections of the poor as "them" and not "us" are public policies which concentrate on keeping the poor out of sight and silent.

To understand the success of these policies it is useful to tackle several crucial questions. Who is poor in the U.S.? Is U.S. poverty increasing or decreasing? What about inequality? Are some groups more likely than others to be poor? What conditions do the poor in the U.S. share with the poor of developing countries? After addressing these questions we can better understand how the poor get marginalized in policy debates and develop more fruitful directions for work aimed at fighting poverty. For statistically describing who is poor this article uses U.S. census figures from 1992 and the official poverty line as defined by the U.S. government. Most who work with the poor feel this line seriously undercounts the poor, but it is the most easily available data.

INCREASING POVERTY

Although it is well known that there was a lot of job growth in the U.S. during the 1980s, there was another trend that is not as well known: the growth of poverty. Throughout the 1960s, the proportion of persons in poverty more or less steadily declined, bottoming out in 1973, at which point it began to increase again. In 1960, 22 percent of all persons were below the poverty level; in 1973, only 11 percent were; but by 1992, this figure had risen to 15 percent. In terms of absolute numbers, there were nearly 37 million people in poverty in the U.S. in 1992, slightly more than in 1960.

❦ Certain groups are more likely to be poor than others—children, single female-headed families, Blacks and Hispanics (the census term). In 1992, the poverty rate for all children under 18 was 22 percent. Children account for 40 percent of the poor, although they are only about 25 percent of the population. A recent study showed that five million children under the age of 12 in the U.S.—one of every eight children in the country—suffer from substantial food shortages. Another six million are close to the margin—either hungry or risking hunger.

In 1992, 39 percent of single female-headed families were in poverty. One-sixth of all households are headed by women, but they accounted for more than half of poor families in 1992.

For Blacks, the story is much worse. A third of all Black persons and more than half of single female-headed Black families were in poverty in 1992. Hispanics fare only slightly better than Blacks; 29 percent of Hispanic persons and 51 percent of single female-headed Hispanic families were in poverty in 1992.

INCREASING INEQUALITY

Not only is poverty increasing, so is inequality. In 1973, the fifth of the households making the least income received 4.2 percent of all income; in 1992, this had fallen to only 3.8 percent. In the same period, the fifth of households making the highest income claimed 41 percent of all income in 1973 and this had risen to 45 percent in 1992. The 5 percent of households earning the most income claimed 17 percent in 1973 and 19 percent in 1992.

Not only are certain groups particularly hard hit by poverty, but poverty is often spatially concentrated as well. If you reside in the central city, you are much more likely to be poor than if you reside elsewhere. While 15 percent of all persons were in poverty in 1992, 21 percent of persons in central cities were in poverty and 42 percent of all poor people reside in the central city. So, you don't just have poor people, you have poor neighborhoods. And the poorest urban neighborhoods are almost all Black or Latino—in fact, Blacks and Latinos are five times as likely as whites to live in inner-city poverty.

If you look at poor neighborhoods, many of the characteristics are very much like a poor country. Urbanists and economists began to draw out this analogy in the 1970s, particularly in reference to Black ghettos. Although poor urban neighborhoods in the U.S. have become more multi-ethnic in the past 20 years, the comparison still holds. William Goldsmith, a professor at Cornell University, writing in 1974, constructed an analogy between the Black ghetto and typical Third World former colonies, describing former colonies in the following way: (1) poverty of material goods; (2) high population growth rates; (3) a few wealthy and many poor people; (4) a small basic industrial sector; (5) low labor productivity, low savings, and little investment; (6) dependence on an export whose supply is not fully utilized no matter how low the price; (7) dependence on imports for consumption, often encouraged by advertising from the exterior; and finally, (8) outside ownership of much of the local economy. In addition, the neocolonialist citizens are restrained from movement to other places by citizenship, language and skills, as well as race, religion and social affinity.

THE GHETTO ANALOGY

Goldsmith goes on to draw out the analogy to the ghetto, one by one: (1) ghetto residents are poor; (2) they have high birth rates; (3) their incomes are highly skewed, a few high and many low; (4) there is almost no basic industry in the ghetto; (5) labor productivity is low, and savings and investment are low, too; (6) the major ghetto export is labor, which is tremendously underemployed, even at low wages; (7) almost all ghetto consumption is supplied from the outside, most of it conforming to outside (advertised) consumption standards; and finally, (8) practically the entire ghetto economy is owned externally. Like the former colonials, and partly as a result of many of these conditions, people usually are unable to leave the ghetto.

Since the time when Goldsmith wrote, another similarity between poor neighborhoods and poor countries has emerged—both U.S. cities and debtor countries have lost control over their fiscal policy.

IT IS HARD TO ESCAPE POVERTY

The poor have taken a particular battering in the last two decades. The undertow is powerful here in the inner city, overwhelming to many of those born into urban poverty, dragging away almost every chance for what the rest might call a "normal" life. A sober reading of our history does not leave much hope. There are more homeless and less housing. Children are born to damaged children. For every mother who courageously drags her children out of despair, two, three, or four others are unable to escape their birth. Anything that might make escape possible—adequate housing, basic education, jobs upon which one can support a family, accessible health care—is absent.

David Hilfiker, *Other Side*, September/October 1994.

In the mid-'70s, U.S. cities experienced a series of fiscal crises which caused lenders to refuse to continue lending to cities unless they adopted austerity programs. Many of the resultant U.S. urban policies look a lot like the structural adjustment policies pushed by the U.S. Agency for International Development, the International Monetary Fund (IMF) and the World Bank, and the effects on poor people in both situations have been disastrous. Human and community services previously rendered at the local level have been slashed and there is a push to privatize remaining services—for example, public housing is being sold off and city services—from health services to education and garbage collection—are being privatized.

A brief glance at two further concepts—uneven development and the distinction between neighborhood and community—rounds out this painful picture.

Poor people throughout the world have been relegated to live on land that is considered undesirable for other uses. However, previously undesirable land may become desirable as the needs of capital change. Capital flows to those places where conditions are more favorable for accumulation. Capitalist development and underdevelopment are two sides of the same coin.

To assess the destruction that involuntary displacement wreaks in the lives of poor urbanites, it is useful to draw a distinction between the terms neighborhood and community. A neighborhood, having a particular location, is made up of buildings and other supporting structures, and occupies a piece of land. It is also a community, which means that it has a social and political as well as physical reality.

In the U.S. capitalist economy, a neighborhood is a collection of commodities. Its land and buildings are bought and sold on the market for profit. As a commodity, a neighborhood goes through cycles in which it is developed, decays, and is rebuilt, cycles that occur in the context of cycles of accumulation for the city and the economy as a whole.

But a neighborhood is also a place where people live, organize themselves, study, reproduce themselves, their culture and ideas, sometimes work, and generally make themselves into a community. The needs of people in communities and the needs of capital do not always coincide, and when they do not, a struggle ensues. From the point of view of capital, a community has a social function, mainly to reproduce labor power and social relations. Black and Latino communities in particular are subject to pressures that maintain significant parts of these communities as cheap labor in more or less permanent under- and unemployment. . . .

THE RISE IN HOMELESSNESS

A growing segment of the urban poor do not officially live in particular neighborhoods—the homeless. In the 1960s and '70s, poor people who were displaced could usually find some sort of alternative housing, often in public or government-subsidized projects. But, during the last two decades, both disinvestment and gentrification cut into the existing housing stock in low- and moderate-income neighborhoods and government cut back on its commitment to build new affordable housing. Whole neighborhoods like the South Bronx in New York were "triaged as a deliberate public policy; that is, essential city services and infrastructure maintenance were withdrawn, banks and landlords in turn walked away, buildings were abandoned and neighborhoods vacated. At the same time fast-growing urban-based service industries attracted professionals back to the city, fueling gentrification and turning neighborhoods upscale and unaffordable for most residents. Throughout the Reagan and Bush administrations, government subsidies for housing rapidly dried up. In this conservative atmosphere, sympathy for other regulatory measures, such as rent control, also waned. Housing costs in most cities skyrocketed as did the shortage of housing units.

Consequently, throughout the 1980s and '90s, the ranks of the homeless have been growing in every major city. Estimates of the number of homeless range from the federal government's conservative figure of 300,000 to the National Union of the Homeless' figure of three million.

RESPONSES TO POVERTY

The response to increasing poverty on the part of many public and private service providers and policy analysts has been to normalize situations which only a few years ago were viewed by most North Americans as intolerable. One example is the growing shelter industry to service the homeless. What was initially an emergency short-term response has become an institutionalized, multi-million dollar a year business which provides jobs to countless middle class workers. For example, in 1987, one state alone, Massachusetts, spent over $200 million for the homeless, approaching $1,000 a bed a month, and this cost has been steeply rising every since. Shelter policies are increasingly custodial and geared to keeping the homeless out of sight, rather than empowering people to take care of themselves. As Kip Tiernan, founder of the first homeless shelter for women in Boston, put it: "Providing shelter is becoming an alternative to providing a decent standard of living for people and the shelter industry has become a self-perpetuating industry."

Another example of how policy analysts are "writing off" the poor is the invention and use in poverty studies and programs of the term "underclass." In the words of Chris Tilly and Abel Valenzuela, writing in *Dollars & Sense*:

> "Underclass". . . has become a stigmatizing and negative label that blames increased inner-city poverty on the ingrained behavior of the poor themselves. Implicit in the term is the notion of a class of people "under" the rest of us, living a life much different from us, even different from that of most poor people. . . .

The most controversial definition refers to underclass members as having "persistent pathological behaviors.". . . . The new focus on the underclass by researchers suggests that the poverty problem is an underclass problem, and that poverty policy is best directed towards correcting the poor's pathological behaviors. Policy-makers who view the underclass as a behavioral phenomenon most often promote punitive programs aimed at discouraging these behaviors, such as . . . stringent welfare work requirements. This distracts attention away from larger social conditions, for example, the need for jobs and affordable housing—the more crucial elements of a program to fight urban poverty.

ELIMINATING POVERTY

Solving the problem of poverty will be difficult, but a first step is making poverty and the poor more, not less, visible. Too many approaches to solving poverty suggest that the poor are themselves the problem; hence the tendency to keep them out of sight and separated from "regular" people as much as possible, whether in homeless shelters, in segregated neighborhoods, in understated statistics or in dehumanizing and demonizing rhetoric. The poor are not the problem; rather poor people have a problem.

Materially poor communities also have resources that need to be tapped. The main resource is the creative energy of economically poor people themselves, especially when that energy is focused towards community development and not just individual development (as is the focus of most so-called anti-poverty programs). So, a critical step toward solving poverty is to adopt community development strategies which rely on the poor themselves as the major agents of change. . . .

People who genuinely want to work to eliminate poverty must develop their ability to work with low-income communities in a way that empowers people in the development process.

| "Billions are hungry and getting
hungrier while a tiny, rich fraction
of the human family stashes away
incalculable wealth."

ECONOMIC INEQUALITY HAS INCREASED

National Catholic Reporter

Many commentators maintain that the gap between the rich and the poor is growing. In the following viewpoint, the editors of *National Catholic Reporter* argue that one measure of this gap—the income gap—is worsening in the United States and in the rest of the world. According to the editors, income inequality in America increased by 22.4 percent between 1968 and 1994. The *National Catholic Reporter* editors contend that this increase has brought the United States closer to the situation found in Brazil, Britain, Guatemala, and other nations with highly pronounced economic stratification. *National Catholic Reporter* is an independent Catholic newsweekly.

As you read, consider the following questions:
1. What neoconservative belief is inaccurate, according to the *National Catholic Reporter* editors?
2. According to Census Bureau statistics cited by the editors, by what percentage did average income grow among the bottom fifth of households between 1968 and 1994?
3. In the editors' opinion, what is the "No. 1 development challenge" of the next few years?

Reprinted by permission from "Gap Between Rich, Poor Growing, Studies Show," *National Catholic Reporter*, July 26, 1996.

$\mathbf{Y}$es, it does matter that the rich are getting richer and the poor, poorer.

While it may be off the political map in the 1990s, the issue . . . will not leave people of conscience alone. It haunts us. Billions are hungry and getting hungrier while a tiny, rich fraction of the human family stashes away incalculable wealth. Morality issues aside, herein lie the seeds of anger, rebellion and destruction. The well-being of the human family and even the survival of the planet is at stake.

PROOF FROM THE CENSUS BUREAU

Two reports published in 1996 solidly reaffirm what we have long known to be true, and belie the neoconservative mindset that argues that all will prosper if governments—with their distributive justice mentalities—get out of the way and allow big business to rule planet Earth.

The first reminder came in June 1996 in a U.S. Census Bureau report written by Daniel H. Weinberg and titled, "Are the rich getting richer and the poor getting poorer?" His answer: Without a doubt.

The Census Bureau has been studying the distribution of income since the late 1940s. According to the report, Census Bureau studies first indicated a growth in the middle class, or, in the words of the report, a "decline in family income inequality," of 7.4 percent from 1947 to 1968. Between 1968 and 1994, however, there has been an increase in income inequality of 22.4 percent.

THE GROWTH OF INEQUALITY

Living conditions of Americans have changed considerably since the late 1940s. In particular, a smaller fraction of all persons live in families (two or more persons living together related by blood or marriage, according to the bureau). Therefore, starting in 1967, the Census Bureau began reporting on the income distribution of households in addition to that of families. By coincidence, 1968 was the year in which measured postwar income was at its most equal for families. The bureau's index of inequality has been growing since, now for more than a quarter-century.

The bureau says inequality grew slowly in the 1970s and rapidly during the early 1980s. From about 1987 through 1992, the growth in measured inequality seemed to taper off, reaching 11.9 percent above its 1968 level. This, however, was followed by a large jump in 1993. The bureau index for inequality in household income in 1994 was 17.5 percent above its 1968 level.

Measured in dollars, the average income of households in the top fifth grew from $73,754 in 1968 to $105,945 in 1994. This is a 44 percent growth. During the same period, the average income in the bottom fifth grew by only 8 percent, from $7,202 to $7,762.

THE RICH-POOR GAP WORLDWIDE

How the average per capita income of the poorest fifth of population compares with the national average per capita income, in selected countries, based on 1993 figures.

	Average Per Capita Income	Per Capita Income of the Poorest Fifth	Average Income of Poorest Fifth as a % of Average Per Capita Income
Brazil	$5,370	$564	10.5%
Guatemala	3,350	352	10.5
Tanzania	580	70	12.1
Britain	17,210	3,958	23.0
United States	24,240	5,814	24.0
Netherlands	17,330	7,105	41.0
Indonesia	3,150	1,370	43.5
Japan	20,850	9,070	43.5
India	1,220	537	44.0
Hungary	6,050	3,297	54.5

Source: United Nations, *Human Development Report 1996*.

Since 1979, the Census Bureau says, it has examined several experimental measures of income. These measures add the value of noncash benefits (such as food stamps and employer contributions to health insurance) to, and subtract taxes from, the official money income measure. The bureau's research shows that the distribution of income is more equal under this broadened definition. "Nonetheless," the report states, "this alternative perspective does not change the picture of increasing income inequality over the 1979–1994 period."

A WORLDWIDE PROBLEM

As income inequality was growing within the United States, it was growing outside as well, according to a report issued by the

United Nations. The wealthiest and poorest people—both within and among countries—are living in increasingly separate worlds, the report states. Moreover, the United States is slipping into a category of countries—among them Brazil, Britain and Guatemala—where economic stratification is most pronounced, with the national per capita income four times or more higher than the average income of the poor, according to the Human Development Report 1996, compiled by the U.N. Development Program.

The ratio of the top 20 percent of American incomes to the poorest 20 percent is now 9-to-1, the study states. "An emerging global elite, mostly urban-based and interconnected in a variety of ways, is amassing great wealth and power, while more than half of humanity is left out," the report states.

The annual Human Development Report was first published in 1990 as a new way to measure countries' progress by going beyond gross national product to factor in life expectancy, education and adjusted real incomes. The report's Human Development Index ranks countries by health, sanitation, the treatment of women and other aspects of life that give what the authors believe is a truer picture of day-to-day existence.

In 1996, Canada leads the index with the most advanced overall human development, followed by the United States, Japan, the Netherlands and Norway. Africa south of the Sahara dominates the bottom.

Among the 1996 Human Development Report's other findings:

• Worldwide, 358 billionaires control assets greater than the combined annual incomes of countries with 45 percent of the world's people.

• Eighty-nine countries are worse off economically than they were a decade or more ago.

• In 70 developing countries, incomes are lower than they were in the 1960s or '70s.

• In 19 countries, per capita income is below the 1960 level.

Finding ways to reverse these trends and move the human family toward more equitable income distribution and a greater sharing of the world's resources is the No. 1 development challenge we face entering the 21st century.

| "The notion of a growing wealth gap, really, is wrong."

ECONOMIC INEQUALITY HAS NOT INCREASED

John C. Weicher

In the following viewpoint, John C. Weicher rejects the claim that the rich are getting richer and the poor are getting poorer. He contends that, contrary to popular belief, the wealth gap between rich Americans and poor Americans has not grown. Weicher asserts that the richest households have owned virtually the same percentage of wealth for over thirty years. In addition, Weicher claims, average wealth has increased significantly. He argues that the press has exaggerated the extent of economic inequality and has performed a disservice by causing a lack of belief in the idea of upward mobility. Weicher is a senior fellow at the Hudson Institute and was chief economist at the Office of Management and Budget (OMB) during President Ronald Reagan's administration.

As you read, consider the following questions:

1. According to Weicher, what percentage of America's wealth did the richest 1 percent of households own in 1992?
2. What was the average wealth per household in 1992, according to figures cited by the author?
3. What dilemma does the latest news of economic inequality create for liberals, according to Weicher?

Reprinted from John C. Weicher, "Wealth-Gap Claptrap," The Weekly Standard, July 1, 1996, by permission.

R emember all the news stories and columns from 1995 about how the rich are getting richer and the poor poorer? Well, you can forget about them—it isn't so.

An Unchanged Gap

Research from the Federal Reserve Board finds that the distribution of wealth did not change over the last business cycle (or, from late 1982, when the economy hit bottom, to the spring of 1991, when it hit bottom again). In 1983, the richest 1 percent of American households owned about 31 percent of the country's total wealth; in 1992, they owned about 30 percent. So the distribution in 1992 was virtually the same as in 1983—and, for that matter, the same as in 1963, when the richest 1 percent owned about 32 percent of the wealth.

The interesting figure is the one from 1992. Until recently, the latest data had been for 1989, and these indicated a more unequal distribution. In 1989, the richest 1 percent owned about 36 percent of the wealth—which sparked that spate of stories blaming Ronald Reagan for a growing "wealth gap." This concern is now out of date, and it may never have been valid. Even if inequality did increase during the long Reagan boom of 1983–89—and that's a big "if"—the increase was completely erased during the mild recession that followed.

About that "if": Every few years, the Fed conducts surveys to determine household assets and liabilities. To discern national patterns, analysts must extrapolate information about 85–95 million households from a sample of 3,000–4,000 households. For 1983 and 1989, they used several methods. The increase from 32 percent to 36 percent—the one so widely reported— was one of the largest that could have been calculated. By most of the methods available, the change in distribution was not statistically significant; by some, the distribution actually became more equal. The broadest measures reveal a clear pattern: a small increase in inequality during the boom, reversed during the recession. The notion of a growing wealth gap, really, is wrong.

Types of Wealth

This comes as a surprise to many people. Mention wealth, and the first thing they are apt to think of is the stock market. There was certainly a stock-market boom in the 1980s, and everyone knows that rich people own most of the stock in this country. So why didn't the distribution of wealth become more unequal? Because stock ownership became more diffuse during that vigorous decade. The non-rich increased their holdings. In 1983, the richest 1 percent of households owned 57 percent of publicly traded stock; in 1989, they owned just under 50 percent; by 1992, they owned less than 40 percent.

THE POOR DO NOT STAY POOR

Economic studies refute the "rich are getting richer while the poor are getting poorer" scenario. . . .

W. Michael Cox and Richard Alm tracked a representative group of Americans to find out what happened to their incomes. The period they studied was 1975 to 1991. . . . Cox and Alm found out that the poor didn't get poorer at all. In fact, only 5 percent of the people whose income comprised the bottom fifth in 1975 was still in that bracket in 1991. Sixty percent of them rose all the way to the top 40 percent of all earners.

Lawrence W. Reed, *Freeman*, June 1997.

What rich people do own, more than anything else, is their own businesses. This accounts for about 40 percent of their wealth. Next in importance is real estate—apartment buildings, office buildings, other commercial property—which comprises about 20 percent of their wealth. Stocks are a distant third, at about 12 percent. The way to wealth, it seems, is to make it, then take care of it yourself.

The distribution of wealth may have remained unchanged during the business cycle, but the amount of wealth did not. The total wealth of American households increased by over $4 trillion between 1983 and 1992, from $15.6 trillion to $19.8 trillion (both measured in today's dollars)—more than 25 percent in nine years. Average wealth per household increased by about 11 percent, from $185,000 to $206,000. These are substantial, and statistically significant, gains in a short period of time.

INACCURATE MEDIA COVERAGE

But press attention to these numbers has been muted. The purported increase in inequality under Reagan got front-page attention, but the recent evidence about wealth has been banished to more obscure pages, or ignored altogether. Also front-page news was a June 1996 Census Bureau report about household income. The headlines blared that the income gap (as distinct from the wealth gap) continued to grow in 1993–94, even though this is just part of a trend that started back in 1968.

In one way, it's fun to observe the reaction of liberals to the latest news about inequality. Those who happily blamed the Reagan tax cuts and social-program reforms for the widening income and wealth gaps in the 1980s are trying to explain why the wealth gap was reversed under Bush, and why the income gap continued to increase in the era of Clinton tax and spending increases, before the Republicans gained control of Congress.

But in another way, it's disappointing that only bad news about economic inequality makes the front pages. What's more, it is a disservice to the public, because the distribution of wealth goes to the heart of what we think about our society. Americans have always believed that they live in a land of upward mobility, where everyone has a chance to succeed. And if we become convinced that this is nonsense—that the rich just get richer, while the poor are permanently barred from improving their lot—then this altered self-image is likely to have unwelcome consequences for our society and public policy.

Thus, the facts—and their dissemination—are important. Yes, the rich are getting richer. And the poor are getting richer. And they're doing it more or less equally.

| "What fails to register in the national imagination is the fact that the vast majority of poor people do work for a living."

THE PROBLEM OF THE "WORKING POOR" IS BEING IGNORED

Katherine Newman

In the following viewpoint, Katherine Newman contends that approximately 30 million Americans work year-round, full-time but struggle to survive despite their efforts. According to Newman, the problems of these "working poor" are largely ignored by poverty programs. The working poor have to cope with a variety of difficulties, she asserts, including taking care of children and elderly parents. In addition, Newman argues that policy makers need to take into account that the problems of working and nonworking poverty are intertwined. Newman is a professor of social policy at Harvard University in Cambridge, Massachusetts.

As you read, consider the following questions:

1. In the author's opinion, why are the working poor ignored?
2. According to Newman, what conditions contribute to disease among the working poor?
3. What has been the result of middle-class economic insecurity, according to the author?

Reprinted from Katherine Newman, "Working Poor, Working Hard," with permission, from the July 29/August 5 issue of *The Nation*, ©1996.

Conservatives insist that poor adults got where they are because they haven't the brains to do better, lack the moral fiber to restrain their sexual urges, or have succumbed to the easy out-of-state support that, we are told, puts people on the federal payroll for having children out of wedlock. What fails to register in the national imagination is the fact that the vast majority of poor people do work for a living. They hold the jobs that no one else really wants: the ones that pay with minimum wage, try the strength and patience of anyone who has ever tried to hold them and subject their incumbents to a lingering stigma. Hamburger flippers, bed-makers, bedpan cleaners—these are the people Jesse Jackson once called attention to when he tried, in vain it seems, to elicit sympathy or at least recognition for the country's working poor.

THE WORKING POOR ARE IGNORED

There are approximately 30 million people in the United States who fill this bill. They are as far from the shiftless stereotype as one can imagine. Their full-time, year-round earnings are so meager that despite their best efforts they can't afford decent housing, diets, health care or child care. Apart from the Earned Income Tax Credit—perhaps the most important antipoverty program of the past twenty years—we've devoted precious little attention to support of the working poor. We have been content to leave them to endure their struggle to survive, even though our best investment in poverty programs might well be to make sure the working poor can stay at work.

It is not surprising that we ignore the working poor. They do not impinge on the middle class; they are not poised to riot; and they are usually too busy trying to make ends meet to argue very loudly for a greater share of the public purse. Theirs is an invisible social problem, but a big one nonetheless. For the debilitating conditions that impinge on the working poor—substandard housing, crumbling schools, inaccessible health care— are hardly different from those that surround their nonworking counterparts.

Indeed, for many these difficulties are measurably worse because the working poor lack access to many government supports like subsidized housing and medical care. Other benefits, like food stamps, are cut off at absurdly low levels and therefore unavailable to people who earn the minimum wage but work a forty-hour week. There isn't much of a safety net spread below the working poor, even though their struggle to survive can be as desperate as that of any family reliant on public support. We have put a great deal of energy into debating appropriate policy for the latter; we seem not to know the former exists.

But exist they do. In central Harlem—where I've done research on low-wage workers—67 percent of households include at least one full-time worker. This, in a neighborhood where over 40 percent of the population exists below the poverty line and 29 percent receive public assistance, is the one number we never hear on the nightly news. The working people of central Harlem often find themselves subject to unstable hours—cut back with no notice because of a business downturn—or seasonal layoffs that hit their pocketbooks hard. Those who are part-time workers, most of whom are involuntary part-timers who would jump at the chance for a full-time position, are denied access to the unemployment insurance system. Hence, when the layoffs come or the hours shrink, there is no backstop save what is left of the welfare system.

The Struggles of Working Mothers

Working mothers everywhere are faced with the problems of balancing the demands of a job and the responsibilities of child care. Poor mothers in Harlem who are working often find that their wages are so low that the best they can afford in the way of child care is of questionable quality and reliability. Even more problematic may be the arrangements for the care of the elderly, whose working adult children may be responsible for their care: There is no money to hire home aides or to make use of nursing homes, the strategies middle-aged, middle-class families turn to (though at great cost).

Employers are less sympathetic, or less flexible, when faced with a store clerk who can't make it in today than they are when a high-priced accountant has to stay home. Vacation pay and sick pay are unknown benefits in the low-wage world. Instead, the working poor are deemed replaceable, and with good reason: There are indeed hundreds of people lining up to take their jobs, particularly in inner-city communities like Harlem, where we found the ratio of jobseekers to successful jobholders is 14 to 1.

Both child care and elder care obligations wreak havoc with the ability of a worker—especially a mother—to maintain her job when catastrophes or even garden-variety problems (the 5-year-old comes down with chicken pox) strike. The frequency with which these problems occur among poor families—working or not—is much higher than among those who are better off. Chronic asthma rates have doubled in the United States between 1980 and 1993, with over 5 million children presently suffering from this dangerous disease. Children in the ghetto are vastly overrepresented among asthma victims; medical researchers are unsure about the reasons. But like diabetes, tuberculosis and other chronic diseases, these are problems of poverty that are rising at alarming rates among ghetto residents. The working poor cannot earn their way out of crowded housing, exposure to toxic substances, inadequate diets and low birth weight babies—all conditions that contribute to disease. These health problems also set the stage for employment instability as parents struggle to cope with the endless rounds of hospitalization and doctors' visits that a chronic asthmatic requires. Many a working mother has found herself forced back to the welfare rolls because she can no longer manage these demands within the strictures of a low-wage job.

Working Women Need Welfare

One of the most troubling trends in the U.S. economy is a sharp increase in the number of people who work full-time but who still cannot, by themselves, lift their families out of poverty; that number rose 50 percent from 1981 to 1994. According to the Institute for Women's Policy Research (IWPR), the problem for many poor mothers is not that they do not work but that the work they can get does not pay enough, last long enough, or provide enough health insurance to enable them to support their families. IWPR research studies found that 40 percent of U.S. women who receive welfare over a two-year period also work, so that in many cases welfare functions as a supplement to wage income.

Dorothy Van Soest, *The Global Crisis of Violence: Common Problems, Universal Causes, Shared Solutions*, 1997.

In recent years a new term has cropped up to describe ghetto dwellers: the urban underclass. Coined by the journalist Ken Auletta in an influential article in the *New Yorker*, the idea took on greater salience with the publication of William Julius Wilson's landmark volume *The Truly Disadvantaged*. The underclass literature paints a picture of the inner city as a public policy nightmare—a racially and economically segregated conglomeration of the welfare-dependent, criminals, broken families and children without stable roots or any understanding of how the employment world functions. Working people are erased from view; they are, presumably, living in better neighborhoods. What's wrong with this picture? There are, of course, millions of poor people on welfare in our ghettos. New York City, for example, has over 1 million people on Aid to Families with Dependent Children (A.F.D.C.). But my research in Harlem shows that no Berlin wall separates the welfare recipient from the working poor. More often than not, both kinds of poor people live under a single roof.

COMBINING WELFARE AND WORK INCOMES

This will not surprise anyone who has ever tried to live on either an A.F.D.C. family budget or the proceeds of a "McJob." Neither will really float a family: Women on welfare cannot possibly pay the rent, the food bill, utilities and other basic necessities (let alone any luxuries) on the stipend provided by A.F.D.C. They have to find additional resources, and most of them do: They work off the books, they receive "in kind" assistance from family members or friends, which has to be hidden from view. The working poor are in the same situation: They cannot pay the rent on their apartments out of the minimum wage. They frequently rely on another family member's subsidized housing and Medicare. America's poorest workers are often intertwined with relatives and close friends who are on welfare. The combination of the two income streams makes it possible to manage the basic necessities of life at a very low level.

Descriptions of inner-city communities that stress a dramatic separation between people who are gainfully employed and those who are on welfare fail to grasp this fundamental connection. This matters because any reforms or cuts the legislature enacts, aiming at welfare recipients, will have a profound effect on the working poor. Any move to rearrange the lives of those on welfare will ricochet back on the working poor. At the end of the day the nation may not be much better off in reducing the costs of welfare: We may simply push one group out and find another waiting on the doorstep. Credible policy begins by understanding how deeply intertwined the two kinds of poverty, working and non-, really are.

America's middle class used to seem remote from the daily problems of the poor. But the massive layoffs of the 1990s have left many a former middle manager scrambling for a job at K Mart where work conditions share some of the features that make low-wage jobs so problematic. Some analysts would see an optimistic aspect to this situation, hoping that the jarring experience of economic insecurity among the relatively advantaged would generate the sympathy, the political will to reconsider the role of government in providing jobs, guaranteed income, health care and the other essentials in life. Most of us who have studied the shaken middle class believe we are very far from that kind of political reawakening. What middle-class insecurity seems to be fostering at the moment is a conservatism designed to punish.

Budget cuts will punish the poor who had the bad taste to get born into the wrong families at the wrong time in our economic and political history. But they will punish the rest of us too: the students who will be shut out of public universities, the elderly who will lose their home health aid (and their daughters who will have to forgo their jobs to care for them instead), the teachers who will be missing from classrooms that have already been stripped of books and pencils, and most of all the children who will inherit a labor market that is worsening steadily and a state sector that refuses to step in.

"The 'working poor' are relatively few and far between, even by official poverty measures that overcount both poverty and work effort."

THE PROBLEM OF THE "WORKING POOR" IS OVERSTATED

Bradley Schiller

Many economists and social policy experts contend that large numbers of people remain in poverty despite the fact that they work full-time. In the following viewpoint, Bradley Schiller argues that existing data misstates the problem of the "working poor" by overstating work experience and understating actual wages. According to Schiller, a single person working year-round, full-time at the minimum wage earns more than the poverty level. He also contends that the working poor are a small minority among families with children. While working poverty does exist, Schiller claims, it is not extensive enough to justify increased government expenditure; instead, he asserts, the government should focus on increasing the poor's work activity. Schiller is a professor of economics at the American University in Washington, D.C.

As you read, consider the following questions:

1. In the author's view, what are the shortcomings in the Census enumeration of income?
2. How are the actual wages of year-round, full-time workers understated, according to Schiller?
3. What proportion of poor adults cite a lack of available jobs as the main reason they do not work, according to the author?

Reprinted from Bradley Schiller, "Who Are the Working Poor?" with permission of the author, from The Public Interest, No. 115 (Spring 1994), pp. 61–72. ©1994 by National Affairs, Inc.

President Bill Clinton's administration has decried the plight of the "working poor" and vowed to create a "worker security" program that will keep every working American out of poverty. As the administration views the job market, it sees 6 million Americans toiling away at jobs yet unable to lift their families out of poverty. . . .

DETERMINING THE EXTENT OF POVERTY

Before embracing [government proposals to address the problem], we should be fairly certain of how widespread the "working poor" problem is. If millions of Americans are stuck in poverty despite extensive work effort, something is surely wrong with the way the labor market functions, and additional government intervention may well be needed. This is the perception advanced by the Clinton administration and regarded as empirical fact by most liberals in and out of academia. What if, however, this perception of the "working poor" is mistaken? What if far fewer Americans actually conform to this perception of working poverty? In that case, the conceptual basis for many worker security initiatives disintegrates and we must look beyond inferred market failure for explanations of persistent poverty.

In principle, any doubts about the actual number of working poor in America could be resolved simply by counting them. As is so often the case, however, the available data sources do not completely respond to the needs of the policy analysis. The resulting information gaps have spawned a lot of creativity in statistical portraits of the working poor. In the process, the perception of working poverty has greatly outgrown the reality.

The perception problem begins with the way the U.S. Census Bureau catalogues work experience and poverty. The annual March Census survey of 60,000 households is the ultimate source of all official data on poverty in America. In that survey, the Census Bureau ascertains (1) the size and composition of households, (2) the total income of households in the previous year, and (3) the extent of work experience of household members. The responses to (1) and (2) determine whether a family will be categorized as "poor." The response to (3) determines whether a household will be categorized as "working poor."

Some of the shortcomings in the Census enumeration of income are well known. The Census counts only cash income, and excludes from its computations all in-kind transfers and capital gains. By excluding food stamps, Medicaid, housing subsidies, and capital gains from "total" income, the Census tends to overestimate the number of poor people and exaggerate their impoverishment. Because in-kind transfers have increased much more quickly than cash transfers since 1960, official poverty counts systematically and increasingly understate whatever success the war on poverty has had.

The Census Bureau itself acknowledges that the neglect of in-kind transfers may result in an overestimate of poverty on the order of as many as 7 million persons (nearly one-fifth of the official poverty count in 1993). To the extent that the "working poor" are closest to the poverty threshold, they are the ones most likely to be overcounted.

A second problem with the official poverty count is the designation of family size. The so-called "poverty line" is actually a series of poverty thresholds based on family size. In 1993, the poverty threshold for a single individual living alone was approximately $7,300, and just under $15,000 for a family of four. In practice, however, the Census compares reported income in the *previous* year to family composition in the *present* year (at the time of the March survey). As a result, growing families (with children less than one year old) may erroneously be counted as poor.

OVERSTATED WORK EXPERIENCE

Other, less known deficiencies in the Census count relate to the depiction of work experience. The first deficiency concerns the source of the data used to identify the working poor. The Census interviewer collects all information about a family's income and employment from a single individual. This "responsible household member" answers all question for him- or herself as well as for all other household members. About half of all the Census data comes from such "proxy responses." Such responses are likely to contain a high degree of measurement error, especially on such critical topics as work experience and income from various sources. A proxy respondent is less likely to recall when or how often another household member worked a short week or was temporarily out of the labor force.

The problem of proxy responses is compounded by the retrospective nature of the Census inquiry. The March interview attempts to ascertain the household's work experience and income during the preceding calendar year. Hence, the respondent must be able to recall the experiences of all household members for as far back as fifteen months. Comparisons of annual Census data to quarterly surveys (the Survey of Income and Program Participation) reveal that the Census responses significantly overstate actual work experience, particularly for low-income and minority households.

The measurement of work experience is critical to assessments of the working poor. Of special importance is the categorization of persons known as "year-round, full-time" (YR-FT) workers. Such workers are widely regarded as the quintessential candidates for the "working poor" rubric. Census procedures, however, may seriously distort perceptions of the number of such workers. In addition to the errors associated with proxy respondents and year-long recall, the Census method for identifying "full-time" work introduces further measurement error. The Census Bureau asks whether an individual "usually" worked at least thirty-five hours per week when employed. If so, the individual is counted as a "full-time" worker. Yet, someone need only be employed thirty-five hours or more per week for a majority of work weeks to be classified as a "full-time" worker. This implies that individuals who often work less than full-time will nevertheless be counted as "full-time" workers. Previous studies of Census data reveal that roughly one in ten poor persons classified as "full-time, year-round workers" actually worked part-time during at least six weeks of the year. Over half of these misclassified "full-time" workers were employed on a part-time schedule for at least eleven weeks of the year.

This overcount of YR-FT workers not only exaggerates the number of working poor persons, but also tends to understate actual wages. As incredible as it may seem, the Census does not ask what hourly wage rate workers were paid. Instead, hourly wages for the prior year are imputed by dividing annual earnings by the estimated ("usual") hours employed. If hours of employment for YR-FT workers are overestimated, then imputed hourly wage rates are consistently underestimated. This problem is endemic to virtually all portraits of low-wage workers.

A PORTRAIT OF POVERTY

Let us ignore for a moment this litany of measurement problems and examine the official portrait of the working poor. There are two distinct groups to consider: individuals living alone and persons living in families (related by blood or marriage).

Although individuals living alone comprise only 21 percent of the poverty population, their reported work experience illustrates some of the measurement problems discussed above. The poverty threshold for a single individual was roughly $7,100 in 1992. According to official Census data, nearly half a million individuals had incomes below this threshold despite working year-round, full-time. Yet, true YR-FT experience would entail at least 1,750 hours of employment (fifty weeks of thirty-five hours each) and more commonly 2,080 hours (fifty-two weeks of forty hours each). Accordingly, *a job paying just the federal minimum wage of \$4.25 an hour would be sufficient to keep any single individual working YR-FT out of poverty.* Yet, the Census says nearly 500,000 such individuals were among the working poor. One must conclude that either the Census depiction of work experience is exaggerated or that these individuals are being paid wages far below the federal minimum.

TABLE 1. WORK EXPERIENCE OF ADULTS LIVING IN FAMILIES

	Poor	Nonpoor
A. No. of adults ages 16–64	13,563,000	121,859,000
Didn't work at all	54%	18%
Worked year-round, full-time	12%	52%
Worked less than year-round, full-time	34%	30%
B. No. of householders in families with children	6,095,000	28,672,000
Didn't work at all	44%	5%
Worked year-round, full-time	17%	77%
Worked less than year-round, full-time	38%	18%
C. No. of married fathers in families with children	2,091,000	23,244,000
Didn't work at all	25%	3%
Worked year-round, full-time	32%	82%
Worked less than year-round, full-time	43%	15%

Bradley Schiller, *Public Interest*, Spring 1994

Most of the policy concern about the working poor focuses on families rather than unrelated individuals. The assumption is that anyone who works year-round, full-time should be able to keep his or her family out of poverty. Table 1 therefore focuses on the officially reported work experience of adults (ages 16–64) living in families. The administration's attention is riveted on the first panel of the table, which indicates that over 6 million adults living in families who worked in 1992 were nevertheless poor. Yet even nonwork is more common (54 percent) than work (46 percent) among poor adults. The contrast with the nonpoor population is dramatic: Whereas only 18 percent of nonpoor persons remained jobless for an entire year, over half (54 percent) of poor persons remained nonemployed. One out of two nonpoor adults work year-round, full-time, but only one out of eight poor persons are reported to be that active in the labor market.

In other words, year-round, full-time work is the exception for poor adults, but commonplace among nonpoor adults.

Most of the concern about the working poor is focused on the plight of families headed by working fathers or mothers. Panel B of the table addresses this concern by focusing on the "householder" (sometimes referred to in politically incorrect terms as "head of the household") in families with children. Nearly one out of two poor families are headed by a nonworker, as compared to only one out of twenty among nonpoor families. Nearly four out of five nonpoor householders work full-time, as compared to less than one out of five poor householders. Here again, the facts are clear: the working poor are a small minority, even among adults who head families with children.

Part of the difference in work experience between poor and nonpoor householders is due to the greater prevalence of single parenthood in the poverty population. A single parent who must assume all child-care and household responsibilities has less opportunity to work full-time than a householder with a spouse. Whether single parents should work full-time also continues to be an issue of intense debate. The last panel of Table 1 sidesteps these issues by narrowing the focus to fathers in married-couple families with children. This is the group that most people would expect to see fully committed to the labor force so as to protect the economic well-being of their families. This isn't the case, however, in the poverty population. One out of four fathers heading poor families failed to work at all in 1992. Only one out of three poverty-family fathers worked full-time throughout the year. These experiences contrast sharply with those of nonpoor fathers, 82 percent of whom work year-round, full-time and only 3 percent of whom remain idle for an entire year.

What Table 1 unmistakably documents is that not working is the proximate cause of most poverty; the "working poor" are relatively few and far between, even by official poverty measures that overcount both poverty and work effort. The labor market might still be held accountable for poverty, however, if it failed to provide the jobs that poor people seek. Although the economy expanded steadily in 1992, the national unemployment rate remained fairly high (averaging over 6.5 percent for the year). Individuals with few skills or experience would have had the most difficulty finding and keeping good jobs.

The poor themselves, however, do not blame the economy for their lack of work activity. Only one out of eight poor adults cite a lack of available jobs as the principal reason for their nonwork. In view of the evident bias in self-reported explanations for not working, this is a remarkably small proportion. Non-working adults in poor families are much more likely to cite home responsibilities, school attendance, or illness for their prolonged absence from the labor market.

Even fathers who head poor families are more likely to blame illness rather than a shortage of jobs for their lack of work. "School or other" is also cited more frequently (36 percent) than job shortages (26 percent) among poor fathers who work only part of the year.

The principal policy implication associated with the phenomenon of the working poor is that the labor market has failed. It has failed to provide jobs to all who seek them or to provide a "living wage" to those who work full-time.

By their own testimony, however, the poor suggest that labor market failures explain relatively little poverty. At most, one could attribute to labor market failure the plight of: (a) those persons who work full-time, year-round yet remain poor, and (b) those persons who work less than full-time or year-round because jobs aren't available.

According to Table 1, there are no more than 1 million YR-FT workers heading poor families. Further computations suggest that there are no more than 630,000 additional householders whose poverty might be explained by a lack of job vacancies. Accordingly, *labor market failure can be held directly responsible for no more than 20 percent of all poverty among families with children.*

THE POOR ARE NOT EXPLOITED

Even this more limited indictment of labor market mechanisms overstates potential market failure. What we counted above was a maximum of 1 million YR-FT working poor householders. A good many liberals are quick to suggest that these individuals are the victims of an unfair wage system. But these workers don't easily fit the Marxist image of an exploited proletariat. Many of the presumed working poor are actually self-employed. Hence, their income status is more a reflection of business performance than the outcome of a bad wage contract. Many others work in the public sector and are likewise not directly subject to private-sector wage determination.

As noted earlier, the Census counts roughly 2 million YR-FT poor workers, of whom 1 million head families with children. Over one-fourth of these workers are actually self-employed. Further examination of the data reveals that over 250,000 poor families actually report negative incomes from a nonfarm business, farming, or rental property. While some of these reports of negative income are probably the product of clever tax accounting, few are likely the outcome of an exploitative wage contract.

Another noteworthy fact is the significant presence of the public sector. Nearly 180,000 of the poor YR-FT workers report being employed by federal (1.8 percent), state (1.8 percent) or local (4.7 percent) governments. Whatever the nature of such employment, surely the resulting poverty cannot be attributed to a direct failure of private-sector wage determination.

These explorations of self-reported employment and income are not intended to deny the coexistence of work and poverty, much less a broader swath of deprivation in an otherwise affluent America. One cannot avoid the conclusion, however, that the Clinton administration's views on the dimensions of the "working poor" problem are seriously distorted. It may be true that over 60 percent of the poverty population lives in families where at least one person has some work experience during the year. The amount of work experience is often minimal, however, and the self-reported reasons for not working are typically personal rather than market-based. Not working is the proximate cause of most poverty. What the country needs to cure poverty is not more worker security programs, but more workers.

The only exception to this conclusion might be those individuals who work year-round but still can't lift their families out of poverty. These prototypical "working poor" householders are an appropriate object of policy concern. There are, however, far fewer of these working poor householders than commonly assumed. No more than 730,000 poor family heads report that they are employed YR-FT in private wage and salary employment. *This represents less than 12 percent of all poor families with children.* This proportion of working poor families would shrink further if more complete information on actual hours of employment and other income transfers were taken into account.

The small core of working poverty that actually exists is worthy of policy concern. The problem is not so extensive, however, as to justify sweeping new worker security initiatives or multi-billion-dollar increases in programs already targeted on this group (e.g., the Earned Income Tax Credit). The most serious challenge for poverty policy is to increase the work activity of the poor, not to restructure the mechanisms of private-sector wage and employment determination. If the administration fails to focus on that goal, it risks not only failing to reduce poverty, but also increasing jobless poverty by imposing more tax and regulatory burdens on private employers.

PERIODICAL BIBLIOGRAPHY

The following articles have been selected to supplement the diverse views presented in this chapter. Addresses are provided for periodicals not indexed in the *Readers' Guide to Periodical Literature*, the *Alternative Press Index*, the *Social Sciences Index*, or the *Index to Legal Periodicals and Books*.

America	"Hungrier in America," May 18, 1996.
Linda Feldman	"Amid US Prosperity, Hunger Grows," *Christian Science Monitor*, December 15, 1997.
Diana Furchtgott-Roth	"Working Wives Widen 'Income Gap'" *Wall Street Journal*, June 20, 1995.
Lowell Gallaway	"Rating the Poverty Rate," *World & I*, May 1995. Available from 3600 New York Ave. NE, Washington, DC 20002.
Issues and Controversies On File	"Income Gap," December 29, 1995. Available from Facts On File, 11 Penn Plaza, New York, NY 10001.
Jacqueline Jones	"American Others," *In These Times*, February 7–20, 1994.
Kenneth L. Judd	"The Growing Gap Between Rich and Poor," *Hoover Digest*, no. 2, 1997. Available from the Hoover Press, Stanford University, Stanford, CA 94305-6010.
Kathryn Larin	"Income Disparities Are Hitting Families with Children the Hardest," *Insight*, February 9, 1998. Available from PO Box 91022, Washington, DC 20090-1022.
Mike Males	"The Real Generation Gap," *In These Times*, February 7–20, 1994.
Stephen Moore	"Focus on Expanding the Economic Pie for All Americans, Not Dividing It," *Insight*, February 9, 1998.
Michael Novak	"What Wealth Gap?" *Wall Street Journal*, July 11, 1995.
Ron Scherer	"Ranks of Homeless Rising as Federal Funding Shrinks," *Christian Science Monitor*, September 3, 1996.
Valentine M. Villa, Steven P. Wallace, and Kyriakos Markides	"Economic Diversity and an Aging Population: The Impact of Public Policy and Economic Trends," *Generations*, Summer 1997.

WHAT ARE THE CAUSES
OF POVERTY?

CHAPTER PREFACE

The correlation between family structure and poverty rates has been studied for several decades. A watershed year was 1965, when Daniel Patrick Moynihan, who was then working in President Lyndon B. Johnson's administration and is now a U.S. Senator from New York, authored a report on the black family in America and the relationship between illegitimacy and the cycle of poverty. Moynihan warned that rising illegitimacy rates in the black community would lead to various social problems, including higher rates of poverty. Moynihan's predictions appear to have come true. At the time the report was released, the illegitimacy rate for black Americans was 26 percent; by 1993, it stood at 69 percent. Moreover, the increase in illegitimacy has not been limited to the black community: The illegitimacy rate among white Americans rose from 2.29 percent in 1965 to 24 percent in 1993.

Statistics suggest that there is a connection between single-parent families and increased poverty. In 1994, the poverty rate for households headed by mothers who had never married was 66.1 percent. Conservative critics also charge that the single-parent family structure results in behavioral problems, contending that poor children in single-parent families are twice as likely to commit crimes as are poor children who live with both parents. They argue that the poverty and misbehavior found in single-parent homes point out the importance of marriage.

While acknowledging that single-parent families are more likely to be poor, others claim that this poverty is the result of economic discrimination, not low morals. They insist that inequality in the job market prevents single mothers from overcoming poverty. For example, the critics assert, the average weekly wage for a female high school graduate in 1993 was $385, compared to $542 for similarly educated men. They also maintain that the clerical jobs that women are more likely to find often pay less than male-dominated industrial fields. Finally, these analysts contend, mothers can be hindered in their search for employment by a lack of affordable child care.

As the rise in single-parent families continues, its effect on poverty will remain a crucial topic among social scientists. Single-parent families and other causes of poverty are considered by authors in the following chapter.

> "The collapse of the family is the most important issue facing American society because it is the root cause of a multitude of other social and economic problems."

ILLEGITIMACY IS A PRIMARY CAUSE OF POVERTY

Andrea Sheldon

Andrea Sheldon is the director of government affairs for the Traditional Values Coalition, an organization of churches that seeks to protect family, church, and biblical moral values. The following viewpoint is excerpted from testimony Sheldon gave before a House subcommittee on welfare reform and the causes of poverty. She argues that out-of-wedlock births create a cycle of material poverty. Illegitimacy causes poverty because children born into single-parent households are more likely to become unwed parents and develop a dependence on government welfare, Sheldon asserts. She maintains that the federal government should seek to reduce illegitimacy through welfare reform. On August 22, 1996, President Bill Clinton signed a welfare reform bill that set lifetime limits on benefits but did not deny cash assistance to out-of-wedlock births.

As you read, consider the following questions:

1. What proportion of children are born out of wedlock, according to Sheldon?
2. How does Sheldon define behavioral poverty?
3. In the author's opinion, what is a powerful factor in the prevention of illegitimate births?

Reprinted from congressional testimony of Andrea Sheldon, *Causes of Poverty, with a Focus on Out-of-Wedlock Births*, Hearing Before the Subcommittee of Human Resources of the Committee on Ways and Means, House of Representatives, 104th Cong., 2nd sess., March 12, 1996.

Today there is a myth surrounding the welfare debate, that there is a safety net worth saving. For all practical purposes there is no safety net. After 30 years and over $5.4 trillion, our country has more children in poverty, more illegitimacy, more teen pregnancies and more urban blight now than any time in our history.

The collapse of the family is the most important issue facing American society because it is the root cause of a multitude of other social and economic problems. It is important to recognize the time lag inherent in many problems associated with illegitimacy, and the effect on American society. The soaring crime rate among urban youths today in large measure is occurring among males who were born out-of-wedlock during the late 1970's. With nearly one out of three children being born out-of-wedlock today, it is obvious that successful welfare reform must reduce the epidemic rate of out-of-wedlock births. The federal government must stop encouraging welfare dependency through subsidizing illegitimacy. In order to have a healthy society, marriage between one man and one woman must be recognized and encouraged.

Two Key Themes

Unfortunately, welfare reform has been sidetracked and now focuses on child care instead of the real issue—illegitimacy. Unless Congress once again brings the focus back to policies that reduce out-of-wedlock births and encourage marriage you will not have fundamentally changed welfare and consequently Congress will have failed to pass genuine welfare reform.

In overhauling the failed welfare system, policy makers must continue to be guided by the following three key welfare reform themes:

1) reduce illegitimacy
2) real work requirements
3) promote moral renewal

I would like to focus on two of these—illegitimacy and the promotion of moral renewal. Halting the escalation of illegitimacy must be the paramount goal of welfare reform and simultaneously, policy makers must promote the formation of stable two parent families. Any genuine welfare reform must reduce the illegitimate birth rate through a family cap.

Additionally, and equally important, the government must assist in the process of moral rebuilding by allowing private social organizations, such as churches and other community institutions, to play a far greater role in educating and shaping the moral code of young people. There is no question that parents, and in particular, low income parents must be given far greater choice in how their children are educated, including the right for their tax dollars to follow their children to the school of their choice.

TWO TYPES OF POVERTY

In her historical study *Poverty and Compassion*, Gertrude Himmel-farb writes:

> After making the most arduous attempt to objectify the problem of poverty, to divorce poverty from any moral assumptions and conditions, we are learning how inseparable the moral and material dimensions of that problem are. And after trying to devise social policies that are scrupulously neutral and "value-free," we are finding these policies fraught with moral implications that have grave material and social consequences.

Robert Rector of the Heritage Foundation has reinforced the necessary role of morality further by talking about two separate concepts of poverty: "material poverty" and "behavioral poverty."

Material poverty is having a family income below the official poverty threshold, and thereby lacking financial resources to meet certain needs.

Behavioral poverty refers to the breakdown of values and conduct which lead to the formation of healthy families, stable personalities and self-sufficiency. Behavioral poverty is manifested by an eroded work ethic and dependency, lack of educational aspiration and achievement, inability or unwillingness to control one's children, increased single parenthood and illegitimacy, criminal activity, and drug and alcohol abuse. There is no question that welfare spending intended to alleviate material poverty has actually led to a dramatic increase in behavioral poverty.

THE CYCLE OF POVERTY

I have seen this in my own work with homeless families who are on welfare. Let me share with you a personal experience.

One day while visiting one of the homeless motels I had a conversation with two women who were cousins, each around 20 years old. They asked me if I had any children and I said no, that I was not married. They both responded almost in unison and without much thought, "Oh, that doesn't matter." What was a very natural response for these two young women made a profound impact on me. These young women had been raised "in the system" and knew every benefit it had to offer. Tragically, these young women were caught in a generational cycle and mentality of behavioral poverty.

Many advocate that welfare is compassionate, when in fact it has really created government dependence with grave generational consequences. What is compassionate about living in a government housing project with your mother, who lived there with her mother. What is compassionate about dropping out of school at age 14 because you have become pregnant, just as your mother became pregnant with you and dropped out of school, and just as her mother before her.

THE BEHAVIOR OF CHILDREN IN SINGLE-PARENT FAMILIES

Children from single-parent families are three times as likely to fail and repeat a year in grade school than are children from intact two-parent families. And they are almost four times more likely to be expelled or suspended from school. . . .

In addition, children from one-parent families have less ability to delay gratification and have poorer impulse control. They also have a weaker sense of conscience or sense of right and wrong.

George W. Liebmann, *Heritage Foundation Backgrounder*, April 6, 1995.

The negative consequences of an out-of-wedlock birth on a child, the mother, the family and society are well documented. Children born into families receiving welfare assistance are three times more likely to be on welfare when they reach adulthood than children not born into families receiving welfare.

Data from the National Longitudinal Survey on Youth show that young girls raised in single-parent homes on welfare are three times more likely to become unwed mothers themselves as girls raised in two-parent, non-welfare families. Tragically, Uncle Sam is the only dad known to 57% of children whose single mothers are on Aid to Families with Dependent Children (AFDC).

REDUCING ILLEGITIMACY

However, those who abide by three simple rules will not be chronically poor in the United States. These three rules for preventing or escaping from poverty are:
- finish high school;
- get a job, any job and stick with it;
- do not have children outside of marriage.

It has been pointed out time and again that no other family in our society, except for those on government assistance, receives an automatic increase in their paychecks for having additional children. Americans are kind and generous people, however, it is clear that taxpayers want to see an end to their hard earned dollars being used to subsidize illegitimacy.

The government must cap the growth of welfare and other spending. Traditional Values Coalition supports the "family cap" provision to cap benefits to mothers having additional children while on welfare. The government must stop encouraging out-of-wedlock births and subsidizing irresponsible choices.

Another means of addressing the increasing rate of illegitimacy is through abstinence education. We must help all youth, and in particular those at risk, to lead healthy, whole lives. Funding should be used for abstinence only education with a focus on those groups which are most likely to bear children out-of-wedlock.

Much of the rhetoric on welfare reform focuses on government solutions to move individuals off the welfare roles without honestly acknowledging the self-destructive behavior that led them to dependence initially.

THE BENEFITS OF RELIGION

Historically, it has been through social and faith-based institutions, not the value-free government institutions, that have best dealt with poverty and despair. In dealing with the growing problems in our society today of family disintegration, substance abuse, crime and despair in low-income communities, there is no question that it is once again the faith-based organizations, churches and synagogues that will be the most effective because only they can take into account the spiritual as well as the physical needs of individuals.

The practice of religion has beneficial effects on behavior and social relations including illegitimacy. One of the most powerful of all factors in preventing out-of-wedlock births is the regular practice of religious belief.

Research by Dr. Richard Freeman of Harvard University shows that inner-city children with religious values are 47% less likely to drop out of school, 54% less likely to use drugs and 50% less likely to engage in criminal activities than those without religious values. Additionally,

- Young women who regularly attend church are roughly half as likely to have a child out-of-wedlock as are those who do not attend church at all.
- Religious belief and practice have also been shown to greatly reduce pre-marital sexual activity among adolescent girls.

- Children aged 10 to 18 who do not attend church are 30 to 50 percent more likely to exhibit anti-social and dysfunctional behavior than are those who regularly attend church.
- Studies show that young people who attend church have a positive effect on the behavior of other youngsters in their immediate neighborhood.

Over the years the government has become increasingly hostile, rather than accommodating, to faith-based organizations in spite of the significant role they play in society. The government's attempts to thwart the activity of these organizations must be addressed and stopped.

THE NEED FOR RELIGIOUS SCHOOL CHOICE

One of the best ways for society to lower the illegitimacy rate is to ensure religious school choice, at the very least for those young people at risk. As we all know, education is about shaping the hearts and minds of children, and inculcating morals and values to these children and what better vehicle than faith-based education.

Traditional Values Coalition believes that the Renewal Community Project co-sponsored by Congressmen J.C. Watts (R-OK) and Jim Talent (R-MO) will be a giant step towards addressing illegitimacy by empowering parents and individuals to move from government dependence to independence. This will be done in a number of ways including through religious school choice. [Also known as "Saving Our Children: The American Community Renewal Act," it failed to become law in 1996 or 1997.]

It is unconscionable that President Bill Clinton, Rev. Jesse Jackson, Senator Ted Kennedy and Congresswoman Maxine Waters, and many other Members of Congress, who have the financial resources to provide private school education for their own children, would deny low-income children the same opportunities of a quality education. For all too many low-income children, religious schools will offer them the best opportunity to a quality education which is their best chance at reversing the cycle that has so entrapped their parents and grandparents.

Mr. Chairman, if we conducted a vote today in this committee on education issues and only allowed those whose children are in public schools or those who were educated in public schools to vote on this matter would we be able to get a quorum?

For too long this great body has tried to hide from any discussions of morality, and as a result you must face a federal subsidy system gone awry and the ramifications of public policy that rewards illegitimacy.

The most important point which needs to be made about the bankruptcy of our current welfare system is that it attempts to treat one dimension of poverty—material poverty—while leaving behavioral poverty to run amok.

Much work needs to be done in our communities and we need to look to each other before we look to HHS or some new federal grant program. The children who are pictured each night on our evening news—children lying shot on some Washington street—are our children—they are American kids.

Each of us as individual citizens need to take personal responsibility for recapturing some part of our country which has been negligently entrusted to government by day and to the criminals by night.

| "Women are being scapegoated by those who blame poverty on individual choices rather than on market forces."

UNMARRIED MOTHERS ARE UNFAIRLY BLAMED FOR POVERTY

Mimi Abramovitz

In the following viewpoint, written before the passage of the 1996 welfare reform bill, which placed a five-year lifetime limit on benefits and established work requirements, Mimi Abramovitz contends that proposals to reform welfare are sexist and punitive toward unmarried mothers. Politicians seeking to reform welfare blame poverty on the behavior of poor women, she argues, rather than on market forces that make it difficult for them to achieve economic independence. Abramovitz maintains that welfare reform measures should respond to the actual lives of poor women and the real causes of poverty. Abramovitz is a professor of social work at Hunter College in New York City and is the author of *Under Attack, Fighting Back: Women and Welfare in the United States* (New York, Monthly Review Press, 1996) and *Regulating the Lives of Women: Social Welfare Policy from Colonial Times to the Present* (2nd rev. ed., South End Press, 1996). This viewpoint was originally given as a speech at a conference on women and welfare reform.

As you read, consider the following questions:

1. According to the author, what is the "theory of the underclass"?
2. What percentage of adults leave welfare within two years, according to Abramovitz?
3. In the author's view, what would be a good replacement for Aid to Families with Dependent Children (AFDC)?

Reprinted from Mimi Abramovitz, "Challenging the Myths of Welfare Reform from a Woman's Perspective," *Social Justice*, Spring 1994, by permission of the author.

U ntil recently welfare reform was not defined in gender terms, even though women have always been overrepresented among poor persons, single parents, and recipients of Aid to Families with Dependent Children (AFDC). [That program was replaced in 1996 by Temporary Assistance to Needy Families (TANF).] Because AFDC has never served women very well, however, it has always been an issue for women. Today's welfare reform efforts—at both the state and the federal levels, and going back to the 1988 Family Support Act—are especially troublesome for women for at least three reasons. First, women are the target of increasingly coercive measures. Second, these measures are gaining support based upon an appeal to misogynist and racist stereotypes of poor women and welfare. Third, women are being scapegoated by those who blame poverty on individual choices rather than on market forces by politicians who use welfare reform to establish their conservative credentials and who substitute the "welfare mother" for Willie Horton in the politics of race. The debate has become very mean spirited and must be reframed if our goal is to achieve social welfare rather than political ends.

BLAMING THE VICTIM

To this end, I wish to identify and challenge current negative messages about poor women and welfare that structure the debate. These messages, which lack solid research support, reflect behavioral theories of poverty, which have become "feminized," if you will, and result in blaming the victim. They also reflect the historic pattern in social policy of rewarding and punishing women based on their compliance with gender roles, misinformation on AFDC's impact on work, families, and the economy, and, finally, society's persistent pattern of blaming women when things go wrong. Current welfare reforms—known as workfare, wedfare, learnfare, and healthfare—are highly punitive measures that have been justified by politicians and policymakers who invoke negative images of women on welfare as culturally adrift welfare queens who prefer welfare to work, live high on the hog, cheat the government, and have kids for money. AFDC is also accused of undermining the work ethic, causing families to break up, encouraging nonmarital births, and leading to other types of irresponsible behavior.

This thinking has been legitimized by the currently fashionable "theory of the underclass," which attributes poverty to the values of the poor, without taking social causes into account. This "culture of poverty" analysis gained ground in the 1980s over more structural explanations of social problems. Unfortunately, its victim-blaming language now dominates the media as well as public consciousness. How often before the 1980s were the poor referred to as "the underclass," poverty as "dependency," and AFDC mothers as "welfare queens"?

The "underclass theory" has also become feminized. Most social scientists describe the underclass as a small, socially isolated segment of the poor, who live in disorganized neighborhoods characterized by high rates of crime, drug abuse, school dropouts, and joblessness. This group is also characterized by high rates of female-headed households, out-of-wedlock births, teenage pregnancies, and welfare use. You needn't listen very hard to hear the message that crime, drug abuse, and school dropouts are among the "tangle of pathologies" that are transmitted from one generation to another by women (of color, it is usually implied), without a male in the house. Such ideas generate support for punitive welfare initiatives by resonating with our belief in rugged individualism, not to mention sexist and racist sentiments. Yet they obscure the real reasons for poverty and welfare use. Personal behavior may make some people poor. Yet can individual choices really explain 39 million people living in poverty or 13 million people on AFDC?

A HISTORY OF PUNITIVE POLICIES

The rhetoric justifying these punitive messages maligns women and fuels race and class tensions. Oddly enough, however, it also contradicts the stated goals of welfare reform. How does calling welfare mothers unmotivated and irresponsible build their self-esteem, encourage employers to hire them, or motivate the taxpayers to pay the bills? It obviously doesn't. Yet the feminized version of the theory of the underclass does reflect the historical practice in social policy of rewarding and punishing women based on compliance with stereotypic gender roles and perpetuates the widespread, but unproved belief that AFDC harms the work ethic, the nuclear family, and the economy.

Today is not the first time in U.S. history that AFDC and poor mothers have been blamed for our nation's woes or received the short end of the social policy stick. From the start, social welfare policy has treated people differently based upon their employment record and on their compliance with prescribed wife and mother roles, rewarding those who conform to idealized versions of womanhood and punishing those who do not. Yet the harshest treatment has always been reserved for the women on AFDC. AFDC was part of the 1935 Social Security Act. It was one of the last of the public assistance programs to be implemented; it paid the lowest benefits, did not include money for the mother until the late 1950s, made suitable home and work requirements conditions of receiving aid, and otherwise tried to drive women off the rolls. Like many of the current reforms, past punitive policies also forced women into jobs at the bottom of the labor market. Federal welfare reforms have typically targeted work. The 1988 Family Support Act (FSA) transformed AFDC from an entitlement program to enable mothers to stay home with their kids to a mandatory work program. President Bill Clinton's welfare plan extends the FSA, calling for more child support from AFDC fathers and more employment from AFDC mothers. Clinton also hopes to "make work pay" by liberalizing the Earned Income Tax Credit and—most controversial of all—by making AFDC a time-limited benefit.

Intentionally or not, these plans to "end welfare as we know it" suggest images of welfare mothers who refuse to work and welfare programs that undercut the work ethic. Yet research and practical and fiscal realities suggest otherwise.

Research shows that only one-third of AFDC recipients are adults, a fact overlooked by those who attack welfare. Of the adults, many already have a work history and are combining welfare with work. The latest figures show that 75% of these adults leave welfare within two years, which counters the notion that everyone is on welfare forever. Moreover, 20 years of research on the relationship between welfare and work has failed to prove conclusively that welfare undercuts the work ethic. Nonetheless, our policy is wrongly based on the premise that it does.

WORK PROGRAMS ARE IMPRACTICAL

On a practical level, the push toward mandatory work programs and time-limited benefits doesn't make too much sense. Welfare mothers work less than other single mothers because they have less education, poorer health, and younger children. High unemployment, the spread of low-paid jobs, inadequate health benefits, and unaffordable childcare also keep many from employment. The recent evaluations of welfare-to-work programs confirm this, in that they show only limited results. This is not a surprise, since corporations are laying off hundreds if not thousands of people daily.

Mandatory work programs also defy fiscal realities. Successful welfare-to-work programs are very expensive and are rarely fully funded. This is an historical pattern, dating back to the 1950s, of promising a whole package of rich services to accompany punitive public assistance programs, but never fully funding them. We got the punitive programs, but not the needed services. This pattern is repeating itself today. Many states have failed to draw down their federal matches and some states, including Wisconsin, have proposed workfare with no services at all.

THE ECONOMIC DISCRIMINATION OF SINGLE-PARENT FAMILIES

Many of the problems [single-parent] families, particularly families headed by women, face are due to low economic status, either chronic or sudden. They also suffer from other socially constructed disadvantages such as the gross inequality in the American educational system, a lack of decently paid jobs for those who wish to work, and a profound lack of community-based services that are necessary to families with two working parents and even more essential for single parents and their children. It is the many forms of discrimination based on gender and race, and the stigmatizing of single women and their children, that play a significant role in their economic, social, and psychological disadvantage.

Ruth Sidel, *Keeping Women and Children Last: America's War on the Poor*, 1996.

Work can help women gain independence, confidence, and control over their lives. However, not all jobs do this. Nor am I convinced that it makes good policy to force women to leave their children for jobs (flipping burgers or mopping floors) when the labor market is already flooded with many desperate people looking for work, and when their children risk navigating drug-plagued and violent streets all alone. Some people justify mandatory work requirements by arguing that other women have to work, so it is unfair for publicly funded AFDC mothers to stay home. To my mind, this reason simply twists the gains of the women's movement, which called for choices, opportunities, good jobs, and sisterhood, not coercion, low-paying work, or divisiveness.

Clinton's package of carrots and sticks is limited to women's work behavior. The states are going further yet by tampering with women's family life on the assumption that women on welfare have large families, produce kids for money, lack parenting skills, and foster intergenerational welfare use. In the name of fostering personal responsibility, women are getting workfare or learnfare with welfare, while some states are making Norplant—the contraceptive implant—a condition of getting aid.

This is happening mostly at the state level, but federal proposals are also being introduced along these lines.

Welfare Reform Ignores Social Conditions

These family-based welfare reforms are not well supported by the data. The typical AFDC family is made up of a mother and two children, and states with high benefit levels do not correlate with more nonmarried recipients. In Europe, welfare benefits are more generous, but teen-age pregnancy rates are lower. The Census Bureau recently reported that poverty is strongly related to marital breakup, suggesting that welfare is not the culprit. The racial subtext embedded in the family values theme ignores that large numbers of white women are on AFDC and the fact that from 1955 to 1988, the out-of-wedlock birthrate for white teens quadrupled while the nonwhite rate, which is higher, grew by a smaller 25%.

The reforms known as learnfare and healthfare target the parenting behavior of poor women. Do we really want to dock the welfare check when the children are truant or do not get their shots instead of dealing with overcrowded schools and the lack of health-care facilities in poor neighborhoods? These parenting initiatives reflect the stereotypic notions that welfare mothers transmit a "tangle of pathologies" from one generation to the next. Yet the data do not support the notion that so many daughters of welfare mothers end up on welfare themselves. If we wish to examine intergeneration of welfare use, we must look at the conditions under which poor women are living, independent of welfare—and must conduct research studies that do not separate the two. Welfare reforms that target family values simply ignore the complex forces in human nature and the social conditions that lead to pregnancy and mother-only families. Many of these social forces are ones over which individuals have little or no control.

AFDC is often viewed as a huge, ever-expanding, and expensive program and is blamed for the deficit and the nation's economic woes. Between 1972 and 1989, however, the caseload held steady at 10 to 11 million, rising to 13.6 million in 1992 due to the recession. The AFDC program has never exceeded five percent of the total U.S. population. Meanwhile, some 47% of all Americans get some kind of government benefit through social programs and the tax code. Meanwhile, the poor are getting poorer and the rich are getting richer. The value of the AFDC grant is less than 60% of the poverty line, having eroded by 40% in the last 20 years.

THE REAL CAUSES OF POVERTY

To conclude, welfare reform is targeting the work and family life of poor women. Since the "reforms" defy research, fiscal, and practical realities, we must ask: What is driving the reforms? It is no secret that welfare reform is serving political more than social welfare ends. Blaming welfare for our economic decline deflects attention from the failure of the market to absorb all those who are able to work and the failure to date of the government to fix the system. Blaming welfare and poverty on the work and family decisions of poor women at the bottom deflects attention away from the decisions made by those at the top, who promote their economic recovery by lowering the standard of living for everyone else.

The welfare mother is an easy target in a society that devalues the poor, women, and persons of color. Welfare reform would look much different if it were to stem from more positive goals. Given the current hostile climate created by the misogynist and racist rhetoric swirling around welfare reform, however, I am convinced that more positive goals will not emerge or survive. For real welfare reform to occur, we must change the debate so that it focuses on the real causes of poverty among poor women and the real problems with welfare.

I wish to add a final thought about new ways of thinking about AFDC. Can we consider replacing it with a program based on the recognition that the situation of poor mothers, like that of many others, reflects a wider crisis in caretaking? The wider issue has already been recognized by family leave, flextime, eldercare, home health care, childcare, and health care generally. These policy developments suggest that the need for caretaking support has become a permanent feature of modern life for all families. What if we were to replace AFDC with some kind of negative income tax or an allowance for all families indexed to the poverty line or even higher, that is not conditioned on work, class, marital status, or family structure? The integration of poor single mothers into a universal income support system based on the need to protect the caretaking capacity of all families could benefit all women and silence the bitter welfare reform debate once and for all.

| "Our forefathers possessed a sense of responsibility far greater than that generally displayed today because they knew no one would subsidize their complacency."

A LACK OF INDIVIDUAL RESPONSIBILITY CAUSES POVERTY

Paul A. Cleveland and Brian H. Stephenson

In the following viewpoint, Paul A. Cleveland and Brian H. Stephenson contend that poverty is caused by a refusal on the part of individuals to take responsibility for their own economic well-being. The authors assert that this attitude is encouraged by government social assistance programs that actually increase, rather than alleviate, poverty. Cleveland is an associate professor of finance at Birmingham-Southern College in Birmingham, Alabama. As of 1995, Stephenson was a student there.

As you read, consider the following questions:

1. How does government income redistribution fail, according to the authors?
2. In Cleveland and Stephenson's view, what were the circumstances faced by earlier generations of American poor?
3. According to Cleveland and Stephenson, how does Eric personify the superiority of individual responsibility?

Reprinted, by permission, from Paul A. Cleveland and Brian H. Stephenson, "Individual Responsibility and Economic Well-Being," *The Freeman*, August 1995.

Despite being motivated by apparent concern for the poor, government efforts to redistribute income have failed. Decades of U.S. welfare programs have failed to rescue both the urban and the rural poor. The only way to maximize economic well-being for all is to rely upon individual choice and responsibility, not income redistribution.

THE TROUBLE WITH REDISTRIBUTION

In order to transfer income to some citizens, government must first take income from others. The more government attempts to redistribute wealth, the less wealth it finds to redistribute. Ultimately, such action consumes capital, depletes wealth, and ends in widespread hardship and increasing despair.

The Soviet and British experiences with redistributionist philosophy serve as excellent examples in demonstrating that redistribution only produces a greater need for redistribution. For example, the English welfare state has led to an unemployment rate of over 10 percent. It is interesting to note that both the rate and the amount of transfer payments have quadrupled since World War II. Thus, as more money is diverted to support more unemployed citizens, more must be taken from the remaining producers in the economy. At the margin, the incentive to work continues to fall and the economy spirals downward.

Some people immediately challenge this proposition. They suggest that eliminating popular social assistance programs would lead to the demise of all concern for the poor. Proponents of government-subsidized housing, welfare, and health care point out the economic value of our poor, and are quick to remind us that America's great prosperity sprang from the depths of our slums. They argue that it was the poor, the uneducated, and the unskilled that came together and transformed this country into an industrial giant.

FAILURE TO SEEK OPPORTUNITY

Making a comparison of today's poor with earlier immigrants is frivolous because our forebears were different from today's poor. The people who came to America in decades past made sacrifices to build a life for themselves in a free country. They abandoned their possessions and embraced the hope of a new land, a new life, and a better home. On the other hand, today's poor are often discouraged and unwilling to seek opportunities. Most early Americans embraced opportunity with hope, but today's poor possess no such general zeal. If we wish to redevelop a spirit of hope among today's poor, we must reject the plea for government-induced equality, and instead replicate the circumstances faced by those who carved out a living for themselves and their families in earlier generations. That earlier reality offered little public assistance. It was market-driven, and those who failed relied largely on the compassion and private charity of their neighbors to help them in times of need.

Mike Ramirez, Copley News Service, reprinted by permission.

Our forefathers possessed a sense of responsibility far greater than that generally displayed today because they knew no one would subsidize their complacency. They carefully considered the choices they made, and lived with the knowledge that they had ultimate responsibility for the consequences of their actions. Too many people today have no such understanding. They live with the assurance that regardless of their actions, government will force society to look after them. This mentality separates them from early Americans. Perhaps a modern example can clarify the issues.

Eric's Story

Eric is a young black acquaintance struggling to improve his life. He is determined to better his situation in spite of his disadvantaged environment and childhood. Eric worked to pay his way through an expensive Catholic prep school, and is currently putting himself through college. His path has not been unscathed and there have been times when it would have been easier for him to quit. For example, last summer Eric was in an automobile accident that almost took his eyesight and his life. During his stay in the hospital, he accumulated medical bills of nearly $10,000. Regrettably, he had no medical insurance.

It would have been easy for a person of lesser character to give up and seek relief through government programs, but Eric did not choose that route. Instead, he chose to focus on his goals, left college for a semester to pay off his medical bills, and then returned to school debt-free and ready to make a better life for himself. Eric's story is significant in that it shows his determination to endure hardship in order to reach his goals. In the process of endurance, Eric's character is being developed and his prospects for future success are being enhanced.

Eric personifies how individual responsibility is a far better foundation for the promotion of economic well-being for two reasons. First, Eric had to recognize that no one made or influenced him to drive, fall asleep at the wheel of his car, and run into a telephone pole, nor did anyone force him to go without medical insurance. These were decisions that Eric made freely, privately, and with the knowledge of their potential consequences. Secondly, had Eric accepted government assistance to remain in school, he would not have learned from his mistakes. People learn the most from their errors when they persevere through the hardship of the consequences that result from them.

THE GOVERNMENT CANNOT SOLVE POVERTY

In addition to these issues, there is the question of equity. The government does not "own" $10,000 to pay for Eric's medical bills. To obtain that money it must take it from someone else. Given the nature of government as collective force, this action is tantamount to theft. No one wins from a long-term system of public theft.

History has demonstrated that government cannot successfully alleviate poverty. In fact, government redistribution actually leads to impoverishment because it promotes the disregard for property rights.

There is nothing wrong with empathizing with the pain and suffering that people endure, or with showing mercy to those who are suffering. Private charity must be responsible so that it does not promote irresponsible behavior. However a problem arises when handouts are presumed to be a right or entitlement. When government force is used to fund charitable activities, the result is a system of public theft which exacerbates profligacy in society. If we truly wish to help the poor and unfortunate we must recognize the importance of individual responsibility, not government redistribution, as the foundation for stimulating economic well-being and character development.

> "The poor . . . are the victims of complex economic and cultural circumstances not of their own making."

A LACK OF OPPORTUNITIES CAUSES POVERTY

Robert C. Lieberman

Robert C. Lieberman maintains in the following viewpoint that poverty is not caused by a refusal to seek work or by a welfare state that encourages perverse values but by a lack of economic opportunity. Referring to the writings of George Orwell, Lieberman asserts that society should offer the poor greater economic opportunities rather than blame them for their poverty. Lieberman is an assistant professor of political science and public affairs at Columbia University in New York City.

As you read, consider the following questions:

1. According to Lieberman, how did the Victorians view poverty?
2. Who should be blamed for society's problems, in the author's opinion?
3. What type of coalition would Lieberman like to see formed?

Reprinted from Robert Lieberman, "Orwell's Poverty and Ours," *The American Prospect*, Winter 1996, volume 24, pp. 90–94, ©1996, by permission of the author and *The American Prospect*, P.O. Box 383080, Cambridge, MA 02138.

" "The very rich are different from you and me," F. Scott Fitzgerald famously wrote. "Yes," Ernest Hemingway teased
Fitzgerald, in a short story of his own, "they have more money."
To Fitzgerald, the rich inhabited a world apart. To Hemingway,
the rich were just like the rest of us, only with nicer furniture.

Visions of the Poor

Today's debates about poverty mirror the Fitzgerald-Hemingway
exchange. "The poor are different," some say. They live in a separate culture, bereft of the values that could lift them out of
poverty. Public policy reinforces their lassitude by encouraging
their morally and socially deviant tendencies. "They just have
less money," reply others. They are regular folks in a desperate
situation, and they behave as any of us would in the same circumstances. Provide for their material needs, or change the incentives that confront them, offer jobs that pay a living wage,
and all will be well.

Something is amiss in these contending visions of the poor—
or, I should say, of poverty, for these views of poor people don't
have people in them, only statistics and myths. These we have in
abundance—reams of tables and figures displaying the extent of
deprivation, and tall tales of "welfare queens" and scam artists
buying vodka with food stamps. But where are the faces behind
the statistics and the mythology, the lives of the poor themselves? In the conservative caricature, the poor remain phan-
toms, ciphers; their individual lives are concealed either by
charts and graphs or by moralistic categories of virtue and vice.
But poverty is brutal and ugly, and it is associated with many
things Americans legitimately fear—crime, drugs, and the apparent breakdown of social standards, especially in cities. Many liberals, too, see poverty through a distorting lens, one that over-
looks or explains away these very real and often uncomfortable
facts about poverty. Some of us posit a false sameness; others see
a dehumanizing degree of difference. What is missing in both
views is a willingness to look hard at the actual lives of the poor.

George Orwell's Writings

No writer has rendered these lives more vividly than George Orwell in *The Road to Wigan Pier* and *Down and Out in Paris and London*. . . .
His reports of the outward effects of poverty—the decrepitude,
the discomfort, the filth—are simultaneously gripping and re-
pellent. But it is his account of poverty's effect on the soul, effects observed from personal experience coupled with keen self-
knowledge, that makes Orwell unique. . . .

Orwell's poor live in a stultifying world, where the basic social and biological functions of life—eating, sleeping, avoiding disease—occupy so much attention that there is little time or energy left for more elevated concerns. The overwhelming experience of poverty for Orwell is ennui. The pursuit of petty vices such as drink and tobacco, the most readily available sources of enjoyment or entertainment, takes on exaggerated importance. When daily life is consumed with such concerns, they become the mind's only focus, and staying alive requires all one's acuity and resourcefulness. "You thought," he writes in *Down and Out*, "that [poverty] would be quite simple; it is extraordinarily complex. You thought it would be terrible; it is merely squalid and boring. It is the peculiar lowness of poverty that you discover first; the shifts that it puts you to, the complicated meanness, the crust-wiping."

But in Orwell's eyes, even the most visibly distasteful of the poor become sympathetic characters. Paddy Jaques, the narrator's "mate" in tramping about London in *Down and Out*, would not be out of place in any American city today. Jobless and homeless, he is lazy, filthy, ignorant, and generally unappealing. He lives in the streets or in shelters, cadging food and tobacco wherever he can. "He had," Orwell writes, "the regular character of a tramp—abject, envious, a jackal's character." Nevertheless, Orwell continues, "he was a good fellow, generous by nature and capable of sharing his last crust with a friend." More generally, Orwell argues that the only thing that separates beggars from "workers" is society's perception of the value of their trade. "A navvy works by swinging a pick. An accountant works by adding up figures. A beggar works by standing out of doors in all weathers and getting varicose veins, chronic bronchitis, etc." When he asks "Why are beggars despised?—for they are despised universally," his answer is simply that, "they fail to earn a decent living." A beggar "is simply a business man, getting his living, like other business men in the way that comes to hand. He has not, more than most modern people, sold his honour; he has merely made the mistake of choosing a trade at which it is impossible to grow rich." Poverty is ultimately humiliating and demoralizing. For Orwell, the detachment of the poor from bourgeois virtues—hard work, cleanliness, self-reliance, and so forth—is an effect of poverty rather than a cause.

THE VICTORIAN SOCIETY

In the 1930s, when Orwell wrote them, these books were more than simply gripping collections of stories and images; they represented an antidote to prevailing Victorian notions of poverty. Romantic and sentimental, the Victorians viewed poverty as an individual failing. The virtues of Victorian society—hard work, responsibility, independence, and the like—were those that would ensure material success. As Fitzgerald believed of the rich, so Victorians believed of the poor: They were different. Being poor was a sign of moral weakness, of indolence and profligacy (the poor were, to paraphrase Stephen Sondheim, "deprived on account they were depraved").

Values Without Opportunities

Despite the overwhelming poverty, black residents in inner-city ghetto neighborhoods verbally reinforce, rather than undermine, the basic American values pertaining to individual initiative. . . . [In a survey conducted by the Urban Poverty and Family Life Study (UPFLS)] fewer than 3 percent of the black respondents from ghetto poverty census tracts denied the importance of plain hard work for getting ahead in society, and 66 percent expressed the view that it is very important.

Nonetheless, given the constraints and limited opportunities facing people in inner-city neighborhoods, it is altogether reasonable to assume that many of those who subscribe to these values will, in the final analysis, find it difficult to live up to them

William Julius Wilson, *When Work Disappears: The World of the New Urban Poor*, 1996.

Oddly enough, all of this moral weakness vanished a decade later when the postwar economic boom produced an era of full employment. The indolent poor of the 1930s became the blue-collar middle class of the 1940s and 1950s. Evidently, they were all-too-willing to work hard for decent wages. What was missing in the 1930s, it turned out, were not virtues but jobs.

This lesson, however, has been forgotten. Modern-day conservatives have once again taken up the Victorian view. The poor are different. They are culturally deficient and morally flawed, an "underclass" whose behavior and values separate them from respectable society. "How does one cope with people who seem unable to advance even their own interests, let alone society's?" asks Lawrence Mead in *The New Politics of Poverty*. . . .

Blaming the Poor

The right thus reduces the problem of poverty to a dispute over the social standards of the poor rather than the opportunities that society presents. As Herbert Gans brilliantly relates in his new book, *The War Against the Poor*, the "underclass" nomenclature perpetuates this view of the difference, and hence the undeservingness, of the poor, allowing the rest of us to revel in our "deservingness." The distinction between "us," the deserving middle class, and "them," the undeserving poor, only reinforces our appreciation of our own virtue.

The right also magnifies the vices of the poor, placing the onus of society's problems on the poor rather than where it belongs, on those with money and power, who set society's priorities and reap society's benefits. The poor, it seems, are neither selfish enough to help themselves nor selfless enough to protect the rest of us. This view of the poor feeds the common misperception that the poor are reaping enormous benefits from government largess. To the residents of Macomb County, Michigan, reports Stanley Greenberg in *Middle Class Dreams*, nearby Detroit is "just a big pit into which the state and federal governments poured tax money, never to be heard from again: 'It's all just being funneled into the Detroit area, and it's not overflowing into the suburbs.'" For these archetypal Reagan Democrats, "Detroit" equals "them"—that is, the black, urban poor who are themselves the source not only of their own misery but of broader social and political ills.

WHO ARE THE DESERVING POOR?

If some conservative critics demonize the poor and emphasize their differentness, others such as Charles Murray posit a false commonality. The poor, for Murray, are at bottom just like us; they respond to economic incentives, based on a cost-benefit calculus. And they would behave like the rest of us, except that the welfare state has corrupted the poor with perverse "incentives to fail" that subvert fundamental bourgeois values such as family, work, education, and deferred gratification. Over time, perverse incentives harden into perverse behaviors and values.

Tellingly, Murray illustrates this worry neither with accurate data (both his arithmetic and his propositions about the effects of welfare on such behavior have mostly been discredited) nor with careful ethnographic observation but with a "thought experiment," namely Harold and Phyllis, his hypothetical young couple in *Losing Ground* who maximize their income by having a child while remaining unmarried and out of work. Murray is also cavalier on the economic benefits to be derived from available work and available wages. In the ghettos of this economy, even Victorian virtue yields Victorian squalor.

In the process of rewarding indolence, Murray contends, social programs dissolved the useful distinction between "deserving" and "undeserving" poor, not by allaying the stigma of poverty but by dragging all the poor into "undeservingness." Welfare, he claims, has made it not only economically feasible but also "socially acceptable" to be unemployed and on the dole. Mickey Kaus similarly implicates welfare in creating a "cultural catastrophe." Aid to Families with Dependent Children (AFDC), he writes in *The End of Equality*, is "the underclass culture's life support system." Whatever its origins, a cultural gap separates the poor, the "underclass," from the rest of us. However they became poor, they remain so because bad incentives have created bad values. . . .

A NEW VISION OF POVERTY

Fortunately, there has been in recent years a resurgence of vivid thinking and writing about America's poor—from the journalism of Jason DeParle of the *New York Times* and Alex Kotlowitz to the stunning ethnographic scholarship of anthropologist Elliot Liebow, sociologist Elijah Anderson, and historian Carl Husemoller Nightingale—that evokes the best in Orwell's work. "Street wisdom," for example, the complex ghetto street culture that Anderson describes, is a set of tools, strategems, and rules of thumb that allows urban residents to negotiate inner-city streets and even to build some semblance of a community on the ruins of urban civilization. For the children of the Chicago projects that Kotlowitz chronicles, the overwhelming fear of violence curtails the dreams of youth and replaces them tragically and prematurely with intimations of mortality and despair. And as Nightingale depicts his young African American friends in Philadelphia, they are hardly alienated from mainstream American values; rather, they are entirely products of those values, almost hyper-American, caught between ubiquitous cultural images of law and order, crime and punishment, violence, and consumerism on one hand and the painful, dissonant reality of their own lives on the other.

All of these writers have sought to approach poverty, particularly the poverty of the urban ghetto, not as a distant and faceless phenomenon but as an immediate and gripping reality that wreaks havoc and despair in the lives of whole neighborhoods and generations. They fall prey neither to the conservative temptation to assume the worst of the poor nor to the liberal instinct to evade the apparent pathologies of poverty. . . . These writers reaffirm Orwell's conclusion that the poor are ultimately human beings no different from you and me; that they are the victims of complex economic and cultural circumstances not of their own making, and the remedies will need to be complex as well. The new naturalistic chroniclers of poverty put the lie to the banalities of the cultural conservatives.

UNITING THE POOR AND THE MIDDLE CLASS

The clarity of Orwell's vision sets a task for progressives who recognize the urgency of addressing the shameful crisis of abiding poverty in the United States. More than at any time in the past sixty years, the American poor and working and middle classes are at common risk. Barry Bluestone calculates that the median working family, given its meager savings, is 3.6 months away from poverty should a breadwinner become jobless. The blue-collar bulwarks of the mid-century boom face increasingly the danger of losing the hard-won gains of their parents and grandparents. Poverty looms for them and their children as it has not in two generations. The time is ripe for a new New Deal coalition, uniting the poor and the working middle class, whose common anxieties and aspirations should be the basis for a powerful political message.

So long as the cultural conservatives set the imagery of the poverty debate with arguments about pathologies of poverty and the moral difference of the poor, they carry the day politically by dividing the sinking middle class from the poor they are approaching. Instead of alliance there is only contempt, relations poisoned by "us" vs. "them" rhetoric that pits Macomb Counties against Detroits throughout the country. As in the 1930s, when Orwell wrote, the poor and the working class share an interest in vigorous government action to create economic opportunity, preserve the dignity and rewards of work, and provide a cushion against what Franklin Roosevelt called "the hazards and vicissitudes of life." But these common interests are obscured, and the promise of liberal renewal is undermined, by the "underclass" rhetoric that casts the poor as the enemy within, rather than as allies in a common enterprise.

The task for liberals is to break down the "us" vs. "them" mentality on both sides of the divide. As a political task, it will require addressing the pernicious racial segregation that still poisons American life. As an intellectual task, it will require recapturing Orwell's soul-searching honesty in addressing the poor as neighbors and fellow citizens rather than as dirty and dangerous scoundrels. For conservatives to call them so—and for liberals to accede—is positively Orwellian.

| "Since the sixties, many of the jobs Blacks have historically held have dried up—a historical sequence so handy that it seems conspiratorial."

DISCRIMINATION CAUSES POVERTY

Mansfield Frazier

Welfare reformers argue that fathers of children on welfare should be required to work to support their offspring. In the following viewpoint, Mansfield Frazier contends that, although he shares that view, discrimination has made finding a job difficult for African Americans. According to Frazier, racial discrimination has resulted in economic policies that have created a permanent underclass. He further asserts that these policies have benefited corporations at the expense of minorities. Frazier is a freelance writer and the author of *From Behind the Wall*.

As you read, consider the following questions:

1. How have whites used economics to exclude African Americans, according to Frazier?
2. In Frazier's opinion, what is the difference between Japanese capitalism and U.S. capitalism?
3. In the author's view, why is life for the American poor surreal?

Reprinted, by permission, from Mansfield Frazier, "Through the Looking Glass," *The Other Side*, March/April 1996.

I heartily concur with conservatives—fathers of children on the public dole should be forced to work and support their offspring. The responsibility should not and cannot be solely on single mothers. But I cannot agree with the mean-spirited solutions now being bandied about in Washington.

Conservatives are not willing to face the fact that there simply are no jobs—and there won't be.

Consider employment for African Americans in this country. Since the sixties, many of the jobs Blacks have historically held have dried up—a historical sequence so handy that it seems conspiratorial. It was as if the racist segment said, "If you make us give you full rights, we'll take away as many of your jobs as we can."

THE ECONOMIC BASIS OF DISCRIMINATION

The vast and rapid expansion of the underclass in the late seventies can be directly attributed to this backlash. Twenty-five years later, it is clear that integration has had little effect on the racist structures of this country.

The goals of integration were quickly subverted as Whites used economics as a basis for exclusion. Making tuition, housing, recreation, and property taxes unaffordable except to certain segments of the population were as effective in halting integration as any segregation order.

When you take into account Federal Reserve policy, job prospects for young African American fathers grow even dimmer. The Federal Reserve requires a 5 to 7 percent unemployment rate in this country. We know what color the majority of those unemployed, potential workers will be.

The economic myth that fuels this policy contends that full employment would result in inflation and that the maintenance of a permanent underclass guarantees the strength of our capitalistic system. The U.S. public has, for the most part, swallowed that argument hook, line, and sinker.

THE SUPERIORITY OF JAPANESE CAPITALISM

By contrast, Japan (also a capitalist economy last time I checked) is at full employment. Japan's businesses are thriving. It even imports workers.

The contrast between Japanese capitalism and U.S. capitalism seems to be that the Japanese are willing to protect their population from unfettered capitalism. Japan has not been willing to leave large segments of the Japanese population out of national economic prosperity.

Consider the recurring trade disputes between the two nations. The Japanese block the importation of apples, rice, and beef in order to protect Japanese jobs and keep prices stable for their own producers. U.S. leaders cry "protectionism!"—as if Japan's concern for its local economic base is a fault.

The Japanese have eschewed the supermarket economy that devours the United States. They refuse to do away with mom-and-pop stores purely in the name of profit. They know these stores provide jobs as well as an essential sense of community. They are willing to pay higher prices for food.

THE POWER OF CORPORATE GREED

In the United States, however, we sacrifice all to the great god of corporate profit. Witness how we export our jobs all over the world for a fast buck.

Have no illusions—when corporate greed has sucked our economy dry from the inside out, our businesses will simply pull up stakes and move to other parts of the globe, leaving us to pick up the fragments.

Let's be clear—when the Federal Reserve mandates 5 to 7 percent unemployment, it is not protecting our economy. It is protecting Wall Street.

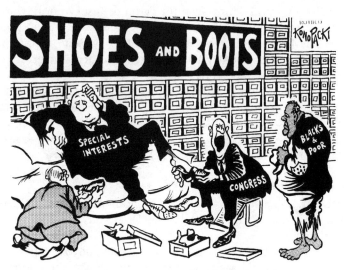

"INSTEAD OF RELYING ON ME, WHY DON'T YOU
JUST PULL YOURSELF UP BY THE BOOTSTRAPS?"

© Huck/Konopacki Labor Cartoons. Reprinted by permission.

Sometimes I feel like a fool. While I was incarcerated, I spent my days earnestly helping other convicts prepare for jobs which I knew didn't exist. When college graduates aren't finding jobs, who is going to hire an ex-con, a struggling single mother, or a young African American father?

Yet even in this dismal climate, I flatly reject excuses like "Why should I bother to get an education when no one will hire me?" That's a cop-out.

PREPARING FOR THE FUTURE

I am over fifty years of age. I haven't had a "job," in the sense of working for someone else, for twenty-five years. I chose a criminal livelihood, and fast, illegal money stopped me from ever owning my own business. If, at fifty, I can work toward establishing my own business, my younger, incarcerated brothers can also.

I told my students in prison that the future belongs to the prepared—and if they fail to prepare, they will find no future. I reminded them that there is a God who will help them, that if they seriously want to go out of this prison and earn a living for themselves and their families, they will not go alone.

I believe this. I try to convince my younger brothers to have faith as well. But it's a tough sell.

One thing is clear to me now, though. African Americans must begin making provisions for ourselves. We must look to our own capabilities, believe in our own abilities, and build our own community-based economies.

BETRAYAL OF THE POOR

When one set of politicians and bureaucrats tinkers with the economy to be sure we never have full employment while another set calls to those mired in poverty to work or else, life for poor people in the United States takes on a surreal, impossible dimension.

Our so-called leaders will betray us. Corporations are too willing to support the current backlash toward the poor. It diverts public attention from the huge profits they make through tax subsidies and unnecessary worker layoffs.

Wall Street is breaking records—but I have learned that means nothing for me as a U.S. worker. Our leaders have bowed down to unfettered global capitalism. Any jobs created won't be here.

To those of us in the underclass, life in these United States has a distinct, through-the-looking-glass quality. If there will be any way out at all, it lies within us.

| "Although [discrimination] exists, it is not a primary explanation for the plight of today's poor."

DISCRIMINATION DOES NOT CAUSE POVERTY

D. Eric Schansberg

In the following viewpoint, D. Eric Schansberg argues that while discrimination does occur in the labor market, it does not lead to poverty. Schansberg allows that two types of discrimination—personal and statistical—affect labor decisions. However, he maintains, an absence of discrimination does not ensure economic well-being, nor does its presence lead to poverty. Schansberg is an assistant professor of economics at Indiana University–Southeast and the author of *Poor Policy: How Government Harms the Poor*, from which the following viewpoint is excerpted.

As you read, consider the following questions:
1. According to Schansberg, how does government policy encourage discrimination?
2. What type of statistical discrimination is used by firms, in the author's view?
3. According to the author, how have Korean immigrants overcome discrimination?

Reprinted, by permission of Westview Press, from *Poor Policy: How Government Harms the Poor*, by D. Eric Schansberg, ©1996 by Westview Press.

The most popular topic concerning income differentials between groups is discrimination. With a controversial subject, it is important to clearly define the terms to be used: Prejudice involves pre-judging something or someone—it is a belief or opinion; discrimination is prejudice in action. Note that in order to discriminate, one must (1) have a prejudice, (2) be in a position to turn the belief into action, and (3) be willing to bear the costs (if any) of those actions. In the context of economics, I will discuss how discrimination occurs in product and labor markets.

Discrimination can also be said to occur when an individual's wages or income is unrelated to his or her productivity and job characteristics. When labor economists measure discrimination, they control for several variables. Whatever remains is considered "unexplained" differences in wages and is designated as (the upper boundary of the extent of) discrimination. There are two types of discrimination: personal and statistical.

PERSONAL DISCRIMINATION

This type of discrimination is the most frequently discussed. Personal discrimination is a matter of indulging one's tastes and preferences concerning the buying or selling of products or the choice of whom to employ. For instance, I might get a kick out of not hiring or promoting women. Or I might decide against buying something from a certain store simply because it is operated by an Asian or a redneck. Or I might decide not to sell a product to people who are black or Jewish. Both parties are cheated out of a mutually beneficial trade because of one party's personal prejudices.

This type of behavior is costly to the one who is discriminated against. However, on average, the degree of competition in a given market and the number of discriminatory firms determines the extent of the cost. For example, in Houston a few years ago, one gas station owner decided to charge those with foreign automobiles a few cents more than the market rate. Since there were many gas stations in the city and only one station was participating, the cost was minimal to those discriminated against.

As long as the discrimination is limited to a few firms in a large market, the one significant result will be some segregation. If a large number of firms discriminate, non-discriminating entrepreneurs have an incentive to enter the market and sell to (or hire) those who have been discriminated against.

In addition, personal discrimination is usually costly to the one who discriminates. To indulge one's tastes and preferences, one may have to turn away good workers in favor of more expensive or less productive workers. The cost of such behavior may temper the desire to engage in it. Remember that discrimination is the willingness to put prejudicial opinions into action. The question may then become: "Do I really want to lower my income in order to discriminate against someone?"

GOVERNMENT DISCRIMINATION

Sometimes government policy encourages discrimination by reducing its cost to zero. When governments regulate a monopoly's prices and profits, they inadvertently provide an incentive for the firm to inflate its costs. If government is going to reduce my profits to "an acceptable level," why not lower profits myself by artificially raising costs? One way to do this is to indulge tastes and preferences concerning others—to discriminate. The cost is zero, since government would confiscate the "extra" profits anyway.

HARD WORK WILL OVERCOME DISCRIMINATION

The civil rights movement must realize that by constantly stressing the problems of racial discrimination and the need for corrective government intervention, the danger exists that their warning may turn on its head and become a self-fulfilling prophecy. If civil rights groups continue to claim that blacks are victims of society, black Americans may come to believe that there is little they can do by themselves to improve their status. But over the long run, the upward mobility of the black population is likely to depend as much on their ability to become self-reliant as it is on their ability to extract concessions from Washington. . . . Those ethnic groups who have relied more on their own initiative have enjoyed the most financial success. When they likewise have stable families, well-behaved and well educated children, and a tradition of pursuing business opportunities, minority groups of all colors have compiled an impressive record of overcoming the hardships accompanying discrimination. Despite the progress we have made in dismantling the worst aspects of racial bias, there is no reason to believe that it may not flare up in the future. And the more self-reliant and financially independent an ethnic group can become, the more successful it will be in weathering the dangers of discrimination.

William A. Kelso, *Poverty and the Underclass: Changing Perceptions of the Poor in America*, 1994.

A more common case occurs when government prevents a market from functioning normally, creating a "market distortion." For instance, a price floor on wages (a minimum wage) creates a surplus of workers (unemployment). With a surplus of unskilled workers wanting to work at the minimum wage, employers can costlessly turn down any particular applicant because there are countless others looking for a job at that wage. The employer can costlessly discriminate because of the surplus created by government. Another example is rent control, which creates a housing shortage. With people waiting in line to get apartments at an artificially low price, landlords can costlessly choose those who fit their tastes and preferences.

Government agencies are generally more interested in maximizing budgets than profits; they have an incentive to pursue (budget) size over efficiency. This inefficiency may include discriminatory hiring practices. If the goal is to expand budgets, bureaucrats may be unconcerned with hiring the best people for the job and may tend to hire less efficient workers who fit their tastes and preferences. (This tendency can lead to discrimination for or against individuals and groups.) Further, their monopoly power can allow discriminatory selling practices. If everyone must purchase a product or service through a government monopoly, there is little incentive to please customers of any type.

Finally, one should note that the greatest problems with discrimination against racial minorities have been caused or perpetuated by government, for example, slavery, police brutality, the Dred Scott decision, school segregation, Jim Crow laws, Davis-Bacon laws, apartheid in South Africa, and religious persecution around the world.

The point is not that government agencies or landlords in cities with rent control always discriminate—or that personal discrimination never occurs in competitive markets. Rather, the point is simply that discrimination is less costly and therefore more likely in markets that are either not competitive or distorted by the government. . . .

If personal discrimination is widespread, enforcement of civil rights laws may be effective. But from economic analysis, we can see that promoting competition and eliminating government's market distortions would be a useful way to curb discriminatory behavior. Finally, because personal discrimination is difficult to prove by its very nature, our energies are probably better focused in areas where we know minorities are hurt on a routine basis.

STATISTICAL DISCRIMINATION

Statistical discrimination is talked about only infrequently, although it is the more common of the two types—we all do it.

That's right—all of us discriminate in this way. When you choose a can of beans at a store, do you select one with a dent in it (if it is the same price as an undented can)? Why not? Do you know there is something wrong with the can? If you are walking alone at night with three boisterous young men coming your way, do you get nervous? If possible, do you choose another path? Why? Do you know that the men intend to harm you? When you vote for offices at the bottom of a ballot, how do you decide? Name recognition? Party affiliation? Incumbent or not? Why? Do you know that the candidates you have chosen are more qualified than their opponents?

These decisions and many others have the following in common: We have incomplete information about the decision, information is costly to obtain, and the choice is of some importance. In other words, people make the best decisions they can with limited and costly information. . . .

The same thing occurs in labor markets. Firms use signals of all types (group information) to do their best in selecting productive employees. Information is far from perfect, gathering information on prospective employees is costly, and hiring ineffective employees is a costly proposition. Thus, firms resort to using grades, college attended, standardized tests, and so on. . . .

Note that neither the employer nor the employee is happy about the failure of these signals to correctly predict productivity. The firm pays the cost of searching for the best people, but sometimes mistakes are made. Likewise, even though particular applicants, say, a student from a less highly regarded university, might be a great asset to a firm, it is unlikely they will be able to signal their ability. Such workers "deserve better" in some sense but will have to start at a lower position to demonstrate their true productivity. Whereas statistical discrimination is "unjust" in an idealistic sense, it is comforting in that it is "nothing personal." People are simply doing their best to earn a living.

FOUR ASPECTS OF DISCRIMINATION

First, racial conflict is not simply a characteristic of the United States in the late 20th century. It is as old as time, it happens all over the world, and it occurs among many combinations of races. We often forget other countries and their histories, but discrimination is nothing new. In fact, one could argue that our troubles in this arena are relatively mild by any historical perspective.

Second, neither political power nor the absence of personal discrimination are necessary or sufficient conditions for economic well-being. Blacks have struggled economically despite substantial political power, including nearly proportional representation in Congress and control of government in many large cities. In the past, the Irish held vast political power, but as a group, their incomes were well below average. Meanwhile, Asians have little political power but have done exceptionally well in economic arenas. Further, Asians have been discriminated against by individuals and even government but have continued to thrive. Thomas Sowell points out that discrimination against the Chinese is legal in Malaysia but that they still dominate the country's economic activity. Although discrimination and political power can influence outcomes, they are not primary explanations for income differentials between groups or economic outcomes for most individuals.

Third, degrees of integration and segregation occur naturally. For example, in dating and religion, people of different ethnic groups pair off and gather together voluntarily in a way that resembles racial discrimination. With respect to housing, people have tastes and preferences that are largely a function of income and independent of race. Thus, because incomes are disproportionately low for minorities, what is in fact a class issue is misconstrued as a racial issue. . . .

Fourth, just as under-representation in a field does not necessarily imply discrimination, over-representation does not imply the absence of discrimination. For instance, blacks make up the majority of players in the National Basketball Association and Asians in the United States have higher incomes than the national average. But it is still possible that individuals in both groups suffer from discrimination. . . .

DISCRIMINATION DOES NOT CAUSE POVERTY

Critics frequently complain about loan-rejection rates for minorities. But they fail to hold "productivity" concerns—for example, default and delinquency rates—constant. For instance, if blacks never default and whites have a 10% default rate, we can conclude that bankers are stupid (avoiding good loans), that they discriminate against blacks, or that they are constrained from lending to blacks by law.

Regardless, one could argue that to the extent there is discrimination, working diligently within an imperfect system is probably the best option. Many Korean immigrants, for example, open inner-city grocery stores. They face some degree of discrimination and a language barrier but have chosen the route of hard work as opposed to incessant moaning about injustices. Many have had economic success. Presumably that option is open to all.

I do not mean to imply that discrimination is a significant explanation for poverty among groups or most individuals. This goes against conventional wisdom. A 1993 Gallup poll reported that 44% of blacks and 21% of whites believed discrimination is the main reason blacks (on average) have worse jobs, income, and housing. Because discrimination is perceived to be so important and because it is a prominent part of discussions concerning the poor, it requires a thorough treatment.

In fact, an overriding focus on discrimination is wrongheaded for two reasons. First, although it certainly exists, it is not a primary explanation for the plight of today's poor. Second and more important, from a practical standpoint, even if it were significant, it would be very difficult to stop. There are plenty of poor government policies we can fix more easily than personal prejudices.

"The distribution of wealth today is nothing but a reflex of the conditions that capitalism creates."

CAPITALISM CAUSES POVERTY

Linda Featheringill

Capitalism causes poverty and an unequal distribution of wealth in the United States, Linda Featheringill maintains in the following viewpoint. She asserts that the capitalist system creates profits for private business owners at the expense of the vast working class. The way to end this economic inequality, she contends, is to overturn the current system. Linda Featheringill is a writer for the *People*, a socialist monthly periodical.

As you read, consider the following questions:

1. According to the author, who are the worst victims of the American economic system?
2. In Featheringill's view, how are profits created?
3. Why are some projects not completed in a capitalist system, according to Featheringill?

Reprinted from Linda Featheringill, "What Causes Poverty?" *The People*, January 1998, by permission.

In late 1997, Peter Edelman spoke in Cleveland. He gained a small portion of fame several months before when he resigned from his post as an assistant secretary in the Department of Health and Human Services as a gesture of protest against the national welfare reform law. He has never claimed to be other than a supporter of the capitalist system, but some of his comments merit our attention nevertheless.

Edelman is well aware that children can be greatly harmed by poverty. He and his wife [Marian Wright Edelman] have been working to ease the effects of poverty for much of their lives; she founded (and still runs) the Children's Defense Fund and he worked with government relief programs for years. Both of them have seen what poverty can do to children.

We of the working class can also see the damage being done to the children of the poorest families among us. They are clearly the worst-off victims of the current economic system, and these small victims are present in every location in the country.

THE DISTRIBUTION OF WEALTH

Edelman argues that inequality in the distribution of wealth is a major cause of poverty. He adds that the situation is getting worse. Twenty years ago, the wealthiest one percent had as much income as the poorest 20 percent of the population; today, that one percent controls as much wealth as the poorest 35 percent.

Edelman may be right about the numbers, but he is wrong about the principle involved. It is not the distribution of wealth that creates poverty. The distribution of wealth is only a byproduct of the system of producing wealth. The system under which the production of wealth and its distribution are organized today is capitalism. Profits—the huge hordes of wealth that fall to the capitalist class—stem from the wholesale theft of labor's product. That theft is possible only because the capitalist class owns and controls the means of wealth production. The distribution of wealth today is nothing but a reflex of the conditions that capitalism creates. It is a byproduct of the class struggle that stems from private ownership of the means of production and distribution, production for profit and the wages system. The distribution of wealth is determined by these conditions. Different conditions would result in different effects. If the means of producing wealth were socially owned and democratically controlled by the useful producers, the distribution of wealth would not be determined by profits and would not be controlled by a small class of owners. It would be distributed in accordance with each individual's contribution in producing and distributing the fruits of their own collective labor.

The Ill Effects of Capitalism

Neither Edelman nor any of the other people who complain about the growing inequality of wealth are willing to publicly acknowledge the fact that the problem is the capitalist system itself. They see the problems caused by capitalism, but they still support the system.

Edelman claims that there is an entire class of people—an impoverished "underclass"—who can't pull themselves out of poverty, in spite of their labor. In truth, all people who must sell their labor power to live belong to one class, the working class. This is true despite different wage levels, employment status, skill levels and other nonessential differences. Just as a man is a man, whether he stands 6 feet 4 inches or 4 feet 6 inches, so workers are workers regardless of the size of their wage, the nature of their skills, their employment or their lack of employment. Pointing out nonessential differences among workers can only magnify their importance in the minds of unwary workers and help to obscure what is essential in defining class. Liberals who harp on the existence of a mythical "underclass" lodged beneath the working class only drive wedges that help to retard the growth of class consciousness.

The Media Aid Capitalism

Over the last two decades, the capitalist class has waged an intense and vigorous struggle to squeeze further revenues from the working class. Certainly, the fears generated by the Cold War served to cover this transfusion, as do the wars against drugs and crime. With the media's compliant cooperation, false or exaggerated dangers are emotionally stressed over the needs for adequate health care, work place safety, education, and security of working people.

Greg Godwin, *People's Weekly World*, October 25, 1997.

Edelman also stated that our economy has never had enough jobs for everyone, even during the good times. This is so. The resources in a capitalist society are devoted to enterprises that will produce profits, and not to projects that will meet our needs. There is so much that needs to be done, there is no need for anyone to be idle. On any given day, there are homes that need to be built or repaired, food and clothing that should be produced and distributed, ecological systems that call out for restoration, etc. There is a lot of work to be done, but not a lot of profit to be made. Hence, things that need doing don't get done.

WELFARE IS NOT A CURE

Now, because he is a supporter of capitalism, Edelman believes that the answer lies in relief programs. He believes in the effectiveness of the welfare system and he predicts that, when everyone is supposed to be kicked off the current rolls in 2002, the government will have to reinstate these programs. (He didn't say what would happen if welfare wasn't put back into place, however.)

We of the Socialist Labor Party have often warned that any pain-relieving act on the part of the government would only be a temporary measure and that welfare payments would not cure the problem. . . . All of us in the working class are stuck with an economic system that steals the wealth we produce and leaves us to try to cope with what is left over.

The theft continues. Thus, we as workers are left with a choice: We can either wallow in our misery and allow the capitalist class to break our spirits as well as our bodies, or we can allow our troubles to inspire us to fight to overturn the system that oppresses us all.

| "The chief cause of black poverty is welfare state feminism."

THE WELFARE STATE CAUSES BLACK POVERTY

George Gilder

In the following viewpoint, George Gilder rejects the common argument that racism is responsible for black poverty. Instead, he blames government welfare and affirmative action programs that he says benefit black women at the expense of black men. He argues that these programs have damaged the institution of marriage and the ability of black men to provide for their families. Gilder is a senior fellow at Seattle's Discovery Institute.

As you read, consider the following questions:

1. According to Gilder, how do black earnings compare to white earnings?
2. How have judges abused the Civil Rights Act, according to Gilder?
3. In the author's opinion, what is the problem faced by the poor?

Reprinted from George Gilder, "The Roots of Black Poverty," *The Wall Street Journal*, October 1995, by permission of the author.

D inesh D'Souza is currently the perplexed beneficiary and victim of an uproar over his book The End of Racism, which emerged in the midst of a momentous furor over the centrality of race in America. Except for the always bravely Olympian sage Thomas Sowell, even conservative blacks have fiercely renounced much of his argument along with his intemperate language. How can anyone deny the power of racism in the face of the taped ruminations of Mark Fuhrman, the rhetoric of Louis Farrakhan, the indignant voices at the Million Man March, the radical split between the races reacting to the acquittal of O.J. Simpson?

I know how Mr. D'Souza feels. In 1979, I published a book called Visible Man: A True Story of Post Racist America. Now this book is being republished by the ICS Press in San Francisco. Visible Man showed that white racism was not a significant problem for American blacks in the late 1970s. If white racism was not much of a problem in 1978, it is manifestly not a problem in 1995.

BLACK ACHIEVEMENT

Neither I nor Mr. D'Souza denies the existence of racial feelings in America and throughout the world. But far from being hostile to black achievement, American whites celebrate blacks at every opportunity. In the truest test, governed by massive voluntary choices in the marketplace, Americans have made the National Basketball Association, 80% black, the most popular sports league, Whitney Houston the most popular and richest American singer, Bill Cosby the most popular and richest comedian, and Oprah Winfrey the most prosperous entertainer. Far from showing racism, American employers, mostly white, have given black women higher earnings, on average, than comparable white women. Between 1973 and 1994, the current-dollar revenues of the top 100 black-owned industrial companies, as listed by Black Enterprise magazine, rose from $473 million to $6.7 billion, plus $4.9 billion in revenues from auto dealerships. Blacks in America have far outperformed blacks in any other society with a substantial black population.

In my view, the most important finding in The Bell Curve by Richard Herrnstein and Charles Murray was that after controlling for age, IQ and gender, the average black full-time worker actually out-earns the average white by 1%. Let the IQ number stand for real educational attainment (as opposed to degrees in easier subjects and from less rigorous institutions), and it is clear that racial discrimination no longer limits black earnings. A more appropriate standard, though, would include a correction for marital status, since married men of all races earn some 30%

more than single men of the same age and credentials. Correcting the Murray figures for marital status gives black men a dramatic edge in earnings over white men. Although such comparisons are full of pitfalls, it is safe to say that black men in the U.S. today earn more, not less, than truly comparable whites.

Rather than admit this reality, the intelligentsia, black and white, would rather pursue fantasies of racial hatred. As I discovered during appearances related to the original publication of *Visible Man*, and as Mr. D'Souza is now learning, denial of racism today is widely seen as evidence of it. In the face of the fury of the charges of bigotry, whites find it easier to go along than to tell the truth.

The Impact of Female Employment

The new competition with black women for jobs has made it even less likely that black men will assume responsibilities as good husbands and providers. Researchers at Pennsylvania State University and the U.S. Department of Agriculture report that among blacks, welfare availability and female employment opportunities are *both* "negatively related to marriage rates." Built upon a perverse logic which seeks simultaneously to advance the interests of minorities and those of women, Affirmative Action actually encourages employers to hire black *women*.

Even when men—black or white—have found employment, the dramatic surge in female employment in recent decades has made it difficult for them to earn what labor unions once called "a family wage," i.e., a wage sufficient to support a wife and family.

Bryce J. Christensen, *Family in America*, October 1994.

Public opinion polls, for example, show that the beating of Rodney King galvanized a newly intense feeling of alienation among blacks in America. Yet anyone, regardless of race, who took the police on an eight-mile, high-speed chase, and then charged at them at the end, should be grateful if he is not shot (rather than beaten). Sensible people learn not to defy or insult police officers who are performing an inevitably messy and treacherous job under tremendous strain. Yet the white media almost unanimously confirmed the black outrage. Today whites indulge the idea of reasonable doubt in the Simpson trial, as if it were possible that a team of policemen would or could contrive an instant frame-up of a supremely popular black athlete.

In effect, all America treats blacks as children who cannot be told the truth. From Harvard Law School deans to ghetto social workers, from the chairman of the *New York Times* to the editors of *Time* magazine, to the steady drumbeat of three broadcast networks, eminent whites are constantly confirming blacks in the crippling comfort of their belief in white racism.

If racism explains next to nothing about black poverty and crime, what does explain it? What is the real cause, so unspeakably unwelcome that it drives opinion toward almost any other explanation, however false or unsavory? The chief cause of black poverty is welfare state feminism. Thirty years of affirmative action programs have artificially elevated black women into economic power over black men.

This regime prevailed from the highest levels of the economy, where black female college graduates with five years on the job significantly out-earned black men in 1991, to the underclass, where a typical package of welfare benefits produced disposable income 28% above a typical job in 1994. It prevailed on college campuses, where more than 60% of the blacks are women. It dominated government job training programs, where girls are found to benefit far more than boys. It even invaded such male bastions as the cockpits of fighter planes, police squad cars, fire stations, construction sites and university athletic teams. In a grotesque abuse of the Civil Rights Act of 1964, judges have interpreted Title IX of the 1972 amendments as requiring academic institutions, in effect, to retrench scholarships and opportunities for superior black male athletes to advance the careers of measurably inferior female athletes, white and black, solely on the basis of sex.

It is an unpopular fact of life that in all societies and in all races monogamous marriage is based on patriarchal sex roles, with men the dominant provider. Welfare state feminism destroyed black families by ravaging the male role of provider.

Some observers claim that black communities benefit from matriarchal institutions. Looking more closely, however, you will find inner cities implacably ruled by gangs of young men, with the "matriarchs" cowering in their triple-bolted apartments in fear of them.

Men either dominate as providers or as predators. There is hardly any other option. The key problem of the underclass—the crucible of crime, the source of violence, the root of poverty—is the utter failure of socialization of young men through marriage. The problem resides in the nexus of men and marriage. Yet nearly all the attention, subsidies, training opportunities and therapies of the welfare state focus on helping women function without marriage. The welfare state attacks the problem of the absence of husbands by rendering husbands entirely superfluous. "Welfare reform" continues the policy, giving welfare mothers new training and child-care benefits and further obviating marriage by pursuing unmarried fathers with deadbeat dad campaigns.

Today, in large American cities, fully 40% of young black men between the ages of 17 and 35 are in prison, on probation, or on the lam; and some 40% of young black women say they have been forced into unwanted sexual activity. To fear young black males has become a mandate for survival on the streets of many American cities. This unspeakable social tragedy—with all its infuriating reverberations on law-abiding black citizens—is the inevitable harvest of government policy.

THE GREAT FIASCO

Even Margaret Mead recognized that in all cultures family values depend on religious supports and male providers. The effort to inculcate ethical behavior and sustain marriage without religious faith is the great fiasco of the modern age. In order to relieve the pain of the poor, our society must come to recognize that their problem is not lack of jobs or lack of money but moral anarchy originating with the establishment and most sorely victimizing blacks.

With both the black and white establishment and even the leading Christian churches succumbing to the siren appeal of unisex policy, what could be more predictable than the emergence of patriarchal religion—however offensive in some ways—as a galvanizing force among black men. If Mr. Farrakhan is deeply culpable for his ethnic fanaticism, surely the entire U.S. establishment is equally culpable for its fanatical assault on family roles. For all races, patriarchal religion has played a central role in human civilization. Patriarchal black churches—from Father Divine's mid-century movement to Christian fundamentalists and Black Muslims today—have served more as part of the solution than as part of the problem of black poverty.

These lessons have become increasingly relevant to whites who imagine that they can sustain a civilization based on secular liberation from monogamous sex roles. As the white illegitimacy rate moves toward the level reached by blacks at the time of the Moynihan Report—and decisively surpasses it in Britain—the events of recent weeks [October 1995] should ring a tocsin for all Americans.

PERIODICAL BIBLIOGRAPHY

The following articles have been selected to supplement the diverse views presented in this chapter. Addresses are provided for periodicals not indexed in the *Readers' Guide to Periodical Literature*, the *Alternative Press Index*, the *Social Sciences Index*, or the *Index to Legal Periodicals and Books*.

Geoffrey Canada — "Cherries for My Grandma," *New York Times*, February 13, 1995.

Bryce J. Christensen — "The Mounting Casualties of LBJ's *Other War*," *Family in America*, October 1994. Available from the Rockford Institute, 934 N. Main St., Rockford, IL 61103-7061.

Family in America — "Broken Families, Impoverished Children," October 1995.

Sarah Ferguson — "The Home Front," *Village Voice*, February 1, 1994. Available from 36 Cooper Sq., New York, NY 10003.

Steven A. Holmes — "For Hispanic Poor, No Silver Lining," *New York Times*, October 13, 1996.

Mickey Kaus — "Bastards," *New Republic*, February 21, 1994.

Heather MacDonald — "Behind the Hundred Neediest Cases," *City Journal*, Spring 1997. Available from the Manhattan Institute, 52 Vanderbilt Ave., New York, NY 10017.

Kim Phillips — "Taking the Heat Off Teen Moms," *In These Times*, March 4–17, 1996.

Barbara Ransby — "US: The Black Poor and the Politics of Expendability," *Race & Class*, October–December 1996.

Charley Reese — "Where's the Justice in Welfare?" *Conservative Chronicle*, March 1, 1995. Available from PO Box 11297, Des Moines, IA 50340-1297.

Carmen D. Smith — "Don't Deny Me an Education," *New Youth Connections*, September/October 1996. Available from 144 W. 27th St., 8th Fl., New York, NY 10001.

Chris Tilly and Randy Albelda — "It's Not Working: Why Many Single Mothers Can't Work Their Way Out of Poverty," *Dollars & Sense*, November/December 1994.

CHAPTER 3

CAN PEOPLE WORK THEIR WAY OUT OF POVERTY?

CHAPTER PREFACE

Most people would probably agree that receiving a paycheck is preferable to receiving a welfare check. Work is often cited as the best way to avoid or escape poverty. This method is especially true for single people because a year-round, full-time job, even at minimum wage, is enough to keep them above the poverty line of $8,050 per year (the line is higher in Alaska and Hawaii). However, what is not clear is whether work is always preferable to welfare.

Those who believe work is more beneficial than welfare note that employment helps people become more responsible and climb their way up the economic ladder. William A. Kelso, the author of *Poverty and the Underclass: Changing Perceptions of the Poor in America*, writes, "If [young uneducated males] work steadily at a variety of low-income positions, it is hoped they will acquire skills and a good work record that will eventually enable them to find positions paying decent wages." Reputable employment is desirable, according to conservative writers on poverty, because it teaches employees skills such as how to follow instructions and how to work well with others.

However, some commentators argue, work is not automatically preferable to welfare. They contend that the low wages and lack of benefits for many entry-level jobs do not make employment a consistently prudent choice, especially for women with young children. Advocates for the poor maintain that because welfare, unlike many low-wage jobs, provides health insurance, it can be a rational choice for someone raising a family. In addition, they claim, the high costs of child care, transportation, and work clothes can leave a family with less money than it would receive on welfare. For work to be a viable option for these families, these critics assert, better wages and benefits are necessary.

In the following chapter, the authors consider whether jobs or government programs can help the poor work their way out of poverty.

| "The typical welfare recipient lacks the skills to find economically viable employment."

SOME PEOPLE CANNOT WORK THEIR WAY OUT OF POVERTY

Alec R. Levenson, Elaine Reardon, and Stefanie R. Schmidt

Welfare recipients, mostly women, do not have the basic skills needed to find well-paying jobs, argue Alec R. Levenson, Elaine Reardon, and Stefanie R. Schmidt in the following viewpoint. Women on welfare have lower literacy levels and fewer years of schooling than nonrecipients, the authors assert. They maintain that these low basic skills put most jobs, including service-sector employment, out of the reach of women trying to get off welfare and out of poverty. Skills training and job training programs are unlikely to enable these women to raise their earnings above the poverty line, the authors contend. Levenson, Reardon, and Schmidt are economists at the Milken Institute, a think tank based in Santa Monica, California.

As you read, consider the following questions:

1. According to statistics cited by the authors, what percentage of Aid to Families with Dependent Children (AFDC) recipients are at the lowest two levels of literacy?
2. How much of an increase in income would level 2 recipients need in order to reach the Los Angeles poverty line, according to Levenson, Reardon, and Schmidt?
3. How do the authors think poverty can be alleviated?

Reprinted from Alec R. Levenson, Elaine Reardon, and Stefanie R. Schmidt, "Welfare Reform and the Employment Prospects of AFDC Recipients," *Jobs and Capital*, Summer 1997, by permission.

In August 1996, President Bill Clinton fulfilled a campaign pledge to "end welfare as we know it" by signing into law the Personal Responsibility and Work Opportunity Reconciliation Act. This welfare reform law changed the fundamental nature of the welfare system. Before the law passed, families could receive benefits for an indefinite period of time. The 1996 law imposed strict time limits on the receipt of AFDC (Aid to Families with Dependent Children) benefits: Adults must work after receiving two years of AFDC benefits and federal funds cannot be used to fund benefits for those who have been on AFDC for more than five years in a lifetime. As if to make the point clear, the name of the AFDC program was changed to Temporary Assistance for Needy Families (TANF).

This viewpoint evaluates the employment prospects of current AFDC recipients who will be forced off the welfare rolls and into the labor force by the new law. We review the existing evidence and present new results from a recently completed report on the employment prospects of current AFDC recipients. We use the old AFDC acronym throughout because that is the more familiar name, and because that was the active program during the period covered by the data used for the analysis.

WELFARE MISCONCEPTIONS

AFDC is a state-administered program that provides cash to poor families with children. The program is funded by both state and federal funds. One in twenty U.S. residents received AFDC in 1995. Some AFDC money supports children in foster care. The rest of the AFDC funding supports families with at least one parent present; the vast majority (91 percent) are headed by single women. Most AFDC families are also beneficiaries of in-kind welfare programs, including Medicaid, Food Stamps, and/or public housing assistance.

The motivation for "ending welfare as we know it" is rooted in the belief that most current welfare recipients are capable of finding "suitable" employment. According to this view, welfare recipients choose not to work because benefits with no time limits provide a disincentive to find work and leave welfare. Cutting off benefits after a fixed length of time is supposed to serve as the much needed "kick in the pants" to get easily employable people into a pool of readily available jobs.

There is a problem with this perspective: The typical welfare recipient lacks the skills to find economically viable employment. Focusing on two measures of basic skills different from formal schooling, we find that typical welfare recipients have extremely poor basic skills. Because of their low basic skills, the vast majority of jobs are not open to AFDC mothers. Those AFDC recipients who succeed in finding employment will end up in low-wage, low-skilled jobs that will not pay enough to lift them and their children out of poverty.

INFERIOR EDUCATIONAL SKILLS

Women on AFDC have significantly lower levels of formal schooling than women not on AFDC. Using a nationally representative data set from 1992, we find that 44 percent of AFDC mothers have not completed high school, while only 25 percent of nonrecipients do not have high school diplomas. Just 19 percent of adult female AFDC recipients have some schooling beyond high school, while 43 percent of other women have such education.

While the differences in education levels between adult AFDC recipients and nonrecipients are striking, the differences in other measures of basic skills are even more striking, especially among women with the same levels of formal schooling. Women on AFDC have significantly lower levels of math and reading skills than other women with the same level of education. The gap in literacy and numeracy is particularly marked for high school dropouts: 88 percent of AFDC mothers in 1992 had poor skills, compared with 76 percent of nonrecipient women who had dropped out of high school.

We calculated these literacy statistics using the National Adult Literacy Survey (NALS). The survey tested individuals' ability to apply math and reading skills to tasks common in daily life. The tasks included a number of skills: reading comprehension, basic math skills, the ability to fill out forms, and the ability to read charts and graphs. The NALS categorizes individuals in one of five literacy levels based on their performance on the test. Individuals at the lowest level of literacy, level 1, are able to do very simple tasks such as locate the expiration date on a driver's license, total a bank deposit slip, or sign their names. They are unable to do level 2 tasks, such as locate an intersection on a street map, understand an appliance warranty, fill out a government benefits application, or total the costs from an order. Individuals at literacy level 2 can perform these tasks, but cannot perform higher-order tasks such as write a letter explaining an error on a credit card bill, use a bus schedule, or use a calculator to determine a 10 percent discount.

According to the NALS scale, most AFDC recipients are at the lowest two levels of literacy: 35 percent are at level 1, and 37 percent are at level 2. The literacy levels of AFDC mothers are substantially lower than those of other women: 21 percent of the adult female population is at level 1 literacy, and 28 percent is at level 2 literacy.

Despite the low levels of literacy documented by the NALS, it probably overestimates the literacy skills of current AFDC recipients. The unemployment rate has declined markedly since the recession of the early 1990s, and those recipients who were the most literate are the most likely to have left AFDC. This means that the current AFDC recipients facing the new work requirements most likely are the "hard core" with lower skills on average than documented by the NALS in 1992.

The Urban Institute also analyzed the basic skills of AFDC recipients, using a different measure of skills than the NALS. Their measure of skills comes from a sample of young adults who took the Armed Forces Qualifying Test (AFQT) in 1979. The military designed the test to predict how well an individual would perform in various military jobs, and has long used the AFQT to screen potential recruits. AFQT scores have proved to be good predictors of success in both military and civilian careers. Unlike the NALS test, the AFQT does not measure an individual's ability to apply math and reading skills to real-life situations. Rather, like many other standardized tests, the AFQT measures the test taker's ability to use math and reading skills in a typical academic context.

Despite the differences in the NALS and AFQT measures of basic skills, the results for the two measures are quite similar. AFDC mothers had significantly lower AFQT scores than other women their age. One-third of recipients had extremely low basic skills, meaning that they scored at or below the 10th percentile on the AFQT. An additional 31 percent had very low basic skills, scoring between the 10th and 25th percentiles on the test. In contrast, only 7 percent of women not on AFDC had extremely low basic skills, and 15 percent had very low basic skills. The Urban Institute skill estimates for AFDC recipients are comparable to our estimates using the NALS (35 percent at level 1 literacy and 37 percent at level 2 literacy).

Short-Term Recipients vs. Long-Term Recipients

The Urban Institute researchers also documented the level of basic skills among women who had been on AFDC for different lengths of time. Contrary to popular perception, a significant fraction (41 percent) of women who have ever been on AFDC have received fewer than two years of benefits during their lifetime. Only about one-third of women who have ever been on AFDC are long-term recipients, having received benefits for at least five years. While short-term recipients have low levels of basic skills, their skills are significantly higher than those of long-term AFDC recipients. Twenty percent of short-term recipients had extremely low basic skills, and 25 percent had very low basic skills. In contrast, 35 percent of long-term AFDC recipients had extremely low basic skills, and 31 percent had very low basic skills.

A LACK OF EMPLOYABLE SKILLS

Few are suggesting that the task of employing those on welfare will be easy. A majority of the current caseload are single women with children, which immediately raises the issue of who will take care of the children while their mothers are working? Just as troubling is the fact that many on welfare have serious skill and educational limitations. For instance, one study found that 61 percent of those on AFDC (Aid to Families with Dependent Children) lacked the skills to perform sales jobs, 55 percent could not do clerical work, and 33 percent lacked the skills necessary for domestic work. As for education, one half of those on AFDC have not finished high school and 38 percent do not read at a fourth-grade level.

William Beaver, *Business and Society Review*, no. 98, 1997.

There is a huge gap between the skills that most AFDC recipients have and the skills that most employers require. Recall that 72 percent of AFDC recipients are at the lowest two levels of literacy in the NALS. We find that over two-thirds of all employed adults in the United States have literacy levels 3 and higher. Even service-sector jobs, reputed to be low-skilled, often require more language and math skills than AFDC recipients possess. Employers typically require their workers to speak and read English proficiently and to be able to do basic math. Much evidence suggests that these skills are becoming increasingly important in the labor market: Employers screen for basic skills when hiring for almost one-third of all jobs in the United States. Low skills make it hard to find a job and even harder to find one that pays well.

LABOR MARKETS VARY

The national statistics on the differences between the skills employers demand and the skills of AFDC recipients do not reflect the fact that AFDC families are not evenly spread out across the country. More than half of welfare beneficiaries live in just a handful of states: California, Illinois, Michigan, New York, Ohio, Pennsylvania, and Texas. The geographic concentration of AFDC recipients means that there may be fierce competition for un- skilled jobs in some cities once the federal work requirements go into effect. For example, one in fifteen U.S. recipients lives in Los Angeles County, where AFDC recipients make up 10 percent of the population.

Analyzing labor markets in different geographic areas pro- vides a more accurate picture of the employment prospects of current AFDC recipients than studying the entire country. In a separate report, we examined the employment prospects of AFDC recipients in Los Angeles County. Focusing on a single ur- ban area allowed us to conduct an extensive analysis of the types of jobs recipients are most likely to obtain, and whether the earnings in those jobs would be enough to raise their families out of poverty, taking into account both the higher wages and higher cost of living in Los Angeles.

We found that, in order to provide employment for all cur- rent AFDC recipients, Los Angeles County's economy would have to create 28 percent more level 1 and nearly 10 percent more level 2 jobs. Clearly, such a huge expansion in the number of unskilled jobs in Los Angeles would require an economic mira- cle. More realistically, many current AFDC recipients, particularly the lower-skilled level 1 recipients, will not be able to find jobs even after they are completely cut from the welfare rolls.

DIM EMPLOYMENT PROSPECTS

If we optimistically assume that all former AFDC recipients could find jobs, we predict that their wages still would not be high enough to lift their families out of poverty. After paying for average-quality child care and other housing and living expenses, we calculated that level 2 recipients would need more than 10 percent more income to reach the Los Angeles poverty line. The situation for level 1 recipients is much worse: They would need more than 30 percent additional income to reach the Los Angeles poverty line. And, relative to the nation, Los Angeles' AFDC recip- ients are much more likely to be at these two worst-off skill lev- els. We calculate that 47 percent of Los Angeles AFDC recipients are at level 1 literacy, and 34 percent are at level 2 literacy.

Taken together, our results and previous research show that AFDC recipients with the lowest levels of basic skills will be most adversely affected by federal welfare reform legislation: They stay on welfare for the longest lengths of time and face the dimmest earnings prospects. A five-year lifetime limit on AFDC eligibility will mean that the lower-skilled recipients will be forced to find paid employment. It will be much easier for the higher-skilled AFDC recipients to find "suitable" employment with or without the new work requirements. However, even if the lower-skilled AFDC recipients find jobs, our results show that they will not earn enough to raise their families out of poverty.

The vast majority of AFDC recipients who find paid work will earn wages that leave their families living in poverty. There are two broad strategies for raising current AFDC recipients' families out of poverty. The first strategy is to improve basic skills enough to raise earnings above the poverty line. Basic skills training could be provided by community colleges, employers, or government training programs. The second strategy is to augment AFDC recipients' income through cash or in-kind transfers.

SKILLS TRAINING WILL NOT WORK

We are pessimistic about the first strategy, basic skills training, for a number of reasons. The 1996 welfare reform legislation does not expand funding for existing basic skills programs for the economically disadvantaged. Therefore, it implicitly assumes that AFDC recipients will gain skills through formal schooling (e.g., through community colleges) or employer-provided training.

Moreover, the federal legislation severely restricts the amount of schooling AFDC mothers can receive. AFDC mothers can fulfill the federal work requirements with up to 12 months of schooling, but they must find employment after that year. One year of schooling is probably not enough to raise the earnings of current AFDC recipients above the poverty line. In particular, we predict that those at level 1 literacy, who cannot perform many tasks commonly taught in elementary school, will need much more than one year of schooling to earn a decent living.

Given that AFDC recipients will be forced to join the labor market with poor basic skills, we expect that employers will be very reluctant or even unable to train former AFDC recipients enough to raise their earnings above the poverty line. Many firms provide basic skills training, but because of the lack of statistical research on such employer-based training, we do not know if it would raise the skills of former AFDC recipients.

JOB TRAINING IS INSUFFICIENT

We are also pessimistic that an expansion of existing federal jobs training programs would improve the basic skills of AFDC mothers enough to raise their families out of poverty.

Evaluation of the Job Training Partnership Act (JTPA) program found that AFDC recipients who voluntarily enrolled in JTPA and were referred to on-the-job-training and job search assistance services experienced large, statistically significant increases in earnings. (JTPA is a federally funded employment training program that targets the economically disadvantaged.) The key to recipients' success was not classroom training, but work experience that helped them learn the skills and work habits needed to hold a job. Nonetheless, the study found no overall decrease in either the amount of government money received by AFDC mothers or the distribution of funds among those women. This is consistent with our calculation that the typical Los Angeles AFDC recipient will not earn enough to raise her family out of poverty, even if she can find a full-time full-year job.

The return to training for all current AFDC recipients may be even lower than the small return reported by the JTPA evaluation. It is likely that welfare mothers who did not volunteer for JTPA would do worse than those who did volunteer for the program. That is because those who did not choose to participate in JTPA have even lower skills than the program enrollees. Mandatory programs that have focused on increasing basic skills among welfare recipients have not had much success in raising literacy levels, and where they have succeeded, they have not then led to employment and earnings gains.

Consequently, if the goal is to keep working families out of poverty, simply forcing current AFDC recipients to find jobs in the current environment will not achieve that goal. Additional public policies will be required. Because the expected success of schooling and training programs is at best uncertain, the surest way to keep current AFDC recipients out of poverty is through public outlays that directly support their standard of living. Possible policies include a more generous Earned Income Tax Credit; housing, food, and child care subsidies; and subsidies to employers who hire former AFDC mothers. Regardless, as has been noted in the public debates over welfare reform, compassionate attempts to move welfare recipients permanently off AFDC could easily, and most likely will, require additional spending that tragically does not seem to be forthcoming.

|"Enterprising Americans can go from the bottom to the top of the heap in short order."

PEOPLE CAN WORK THEIR WAY INTO WEALTH

Kenneth R. Weinstein

In the following viewpoint, Kenneth R. Weinstein contends that, contrary to popular opinion, Americans can become wealthy through hard work. Weinstein argues that entry-level jobs and determination can be the stepping stones to economic success. He maintains that other Americans can replicate the success of rags-to-riches stories if the government does not interfere with the commercial activities of the nation. Weinstein is the director of the Government Reform Project at the Heritage Foundation, a research and educational think tank that promotes free enterprise, limited government, and other conservative public policies.

As you read, consider the following questions:

1. What are "PSDs," according to the author?
2. According to Weinstein, what industry has created many success stories?
3. What are the "three Cs to individual achievement," according to J.B. Fuqua, as quoted by the author?

Reprinted from Kenneth R. Weinstein, "From Peon to Boss: It Still Happens," *The American Enterprise*, July/August 1997, with permission from *The American Enterprise*, a Washington-based magazine of politics, business, and culture, July/August 1997.

A ndrew Carnegie started out as a $1.20 a week bobbin boy. By the end of his life he was head of the largest company in the world. Rags to riches, literally, in one working career.

But that was the old, freewheeling, frontier America. Today, we're told that you need a fancy education and a friend at the bank to make it big. Books and news stories say upward mobility ended with the last generation. The U.S. is becoming a caste society. Now, it's only the rich who get richer.

Is Horatio Alger dead? The nineteenth-century Unitarian minister, made famous by his 130 tales of up-from-nothing success, once inspired generations of Americans. Nowadays, he is mocked as a myth-maker. Sophisticates sneer at the idea that big things can be achieved through hard work alone. It's a nice notion, they say, but it can't be done today. Only the well-credentialed and the already-well-off can hope to break through.

HARD WORK IS STILL EFFECTIVE

Such pessimism is factually unfounded and ultimately self-defeating. In the 1990s just as in the nineteenth century, enterprising Americans can go from the bottom to the top of the heap in short order.

In an 1859 address, Abraham Lincoln, himself a model of the poor-but-ambitious American, attacked the view that "whoever is once a hired laborer, is fatally fixed in that condition for life." "The prudent, penniless beginner," Lincoln noted, "labors for wages awhile, saves a surplus with which to buy tools or land for himself," and eventually saves enough to hire others to help him. These hired laborers then begin the same cycle over again. This, Lincoln proclaimed, was a "just and generous, and prosperous system, which opens the way for all—gives hope to all, and energy, and progress, and the improvement of condition to all."

Today there is actually a Horatio Alger Association of Distinguished Americans, based in Alexandria, Virginia, that recognizes individuals who have "risen from humble beginnings to personify the ideal of success through hard work and courage." The society was formed a half-century ago to teach young people that America's days of opportunity are not over.

SUCCESS STORIES

One of the 1997 Alger inductees is Alan "Ace" Greenberg. As a young man in Depression-era Oklahoma City, Greenberg read *The Robber Barons* and decided that he, too, would end up on Wall Street. In 1949, after graduating from the University of Missouri, he headed East and landed a $32.50 a week job as a clerk in the oil department of the brokerage house Bear Stearns. Six months later, he became an arbitrage clerk. By age 25, he was running the arbitrage department before becoming a Bear Stearns partner at age 31. Soon diagnosed with cancer, he triumphed over it—and over his competitors—guided by the belief that "thou will do well in commerce as long as thou dost not believe thine own odor is perfume."

In 1978, "Ace" was made CEO of Bear Stearns. Under his reign, the company grew from 1,200 employees to 7,800. And while other brokerage firms were busy recruiting MBAs, Greenberg declared an abiding preference for "PSDs"—Poor, Smart, with a deep Desire to be rich, and no college education at all.

The historian Henry Adams (1838–1918) noted that in the United States, "the penniless and homeless Scotch and Irish immigrant was caught and consumed" by economic opportunity. "Every stroke of the axe and the hoe made him a capitalist, and made gentlemen of his children."

The members of the billionaire club at the top of the *Forbes* 400 list of the wealthiest Americans may not all be gentlemen, but there are certainly more than a few high school and college dropouts who were "penniless beginners" laboring for others as they saved enough to build their own businesses. Takeover titan Kirk Kerkorian (worth $3.4 billion) didn't make it through junior high, but started a charter airline company as a World War II veteran using surplus planes. Lawrence Ellison ($6 billion) quit the University of Illinois and struggled through low-level jobs in Silicon Valley before starting network computer manufacturer Oracle with just $1,850 in 1973. Entrepreneur Wayne Huizenga started with a used garbage truck in 1962 and ended up with $1.4 billion in 1996. Alfred Lerner ($1.4 billion) began professional life as a $75 a week furniture salesman, but squirreled away enough cash to buy a 59-unit apartment building in Cleveland that was the start of his massive real estate and banking holdings. Carl Lindner of American Financial ($1.1 billion) was a high school dropout who opened an ice cream parlor in 1940 with $1,200 in savings.

HUMBLE BEGINNINGS

Even at today's biggest companies there are lots of chief executives who began at those same firms in the humblest entry-level positions. General Motors chairman John Smith began with GM in the early 1960s as an assembly line worker. Ivan Seidenberg, CEO of NYNEX, started as a cable splicer's assistant at $89.50 a week. Darryl Hartley-Leonard rose from desk clerk to become

CEO at Hyatt Hotels. Edward Rensi, president of McDonald's USA, was an 85-cents-an-hour counter worker at a golden arches restaurant in the beginning.

Not only at the business apex but all across America one can find men and women who have sharply improved their fortunes via our wide open business system. Take Herman J. Russell. He started shining shoes at eight, took a paper route when he was ten, saved money at the suggestion of his father, and eventually built up one of Atlanta's largest construction and property management companies. With more than 1,400 employees and $164 million in sales, his company is one of the larger black-owned enterprises in the country.

HARD WORK PAYS OFF

Roberto Suarez fled Cuba after Castro came to power and arrived in Miami with just $5 in his pocket and a small duffel bag of clothes. He doggedly pursued every job lead. When he heard about openings at "the Herald," he had no idea what it was, but he went there anyway and stood in line for hours, hoping to be called for temporary work. Eventually he was picked for a 10-hour night shift bundling newspapers. Leaving work at 5 A.M., he was told to come back in five hours if he wanted to work again. He returned every day; after three months he was given a regular five-day shift. Suarez went on to become president of the Miami Herald Publishing Co.

Daniel Levine, *Policy Review*, May/June 1997.

Too many young people today are "not willing to wait or pay the price" necessary for success, Russell argues. He says too many blacks, in particular, have given up on blue-collar jobs as a path to economic success. "You don't have to have a white-collar job to be successful in life," he says. "When I was serving my apprenticeship, most of my peers were black Americans. But we don't see that today."

In many places, the faces you'll now see behind the counters of entry-level businesses are those of immigrants. Charlie Chea, 44, lost both of his parents and eight of his nine sisters to the Khmer Rouge terror that swept Cambodia after the U.S. withdrawal from southeast Asia. Chea somehow escaped and, in 1973, made it to the U.S. He scrimped and saved for nine years. Then in 1982, with $30,000 in the bank, Chea and his wife bought a 50-foot boat and formed the Captain Charlie Seafood Company in Houston. The business quickly grew to a fleet of 30 boats, but fishing on the Gulf Coast took a turn for the worse—and some of his fishermen proved less than trustworthy, keeping much of the catch for themselves. So Chea re-grouped, swapped his boats for a fleet of 15 trucks, and Captain Charlie became one of the leading distributors of seafood in Texas, Alabama, Louisiana, Mississippi, and Oklahoma.

Fifteen years after Chea came to Houston, Captain Charlie Seafood now has annual sales of over $30 million. "If you are honest and work hard," Chea says with enthusiasm, "you can be a success." He worries some Americans have become too big for their britches and are unwilling to start humbly and work their way up. When thinking about some successful businessman in the future, he suggests, remember that "many of these guys were 'truck drivers,' too, at some point."

THE SUCCESS OF THE TRUCKING INDUSTRY

In point of fact, few industries boast more entrepreneurial success stories than trucking. Deregulation of the industry in the 1980s caused thousands of new companies to spring up, including 20 or so brand new launches that now do over $100 million in business annually. The owners of lots of today's largest companies were once shift drivers who saved enough money to buy their own rigs and then build their own fleets.

One such success story is the current chairman of the U.S. Chamber of Commerce, Michael Starnes. Starnes started driving a delivery truck, worked as a sales rep for a big trucking company, then managed operations for a smaller outfit. In 1978, at age 33, Starnes and his wife formed M.S. Carriers, with $10,000 in savings and a $20,000 line of credit. For the first half-year, they ran this one-truck operation out of a bedroom in their Memphis home. M.S. Carriers quickly grew to 50 trucks.

By 1986, M.S. Carriers had $35 million in annual revenues and 250 trucks. Now, two decades later, it has 2,500 trucks serving the U.S., Canada, and Mexico, employs 3,300 workers, and grosses nearly $400 million a year.

IRA LIPMAN'S STORY

Spare rooms in Memphis homes seem to be good places to start up multimillion-dollar corporations. Ira Lipman's 12,000-person business was launched underground—in his basement. Back when he was just eight years old and growing up in Little Rock, Arkansas, Lipman began working for his father's detective agency, testing store clerks to see if they would give the proper change to a child. Lipman honed his sleuthing skills and amidst the historic desegregation of Little Rock's Central High School in 1957, the 16-year-old became NBC reporter John Chancellor's main source inside the school. (Lest one think social mobility in America is a one-way street, note that Arkansas Governor Orval Faubus, who fought the desegregation order from President Eisenhower, ended life as a $60 a week bank teller.)

After a couple years of college, Lipman took a job as a salesman for his father's gumshoe agency and quickly tripled its $100,000 earnings. But when several clients asked the firm to provide guard services, Lipman's father balked. Sensing an opportunity, Ira borrowed $1,000 from his father in 1963 and started his own security guard service. Today, Guardsmark is the nation's fifth-largest security firm, with $200 million in revenues and 12,000 employees. Lipman feels a real debt to America: "I'm unabashedly proud of this country. I've seen it grow from 125 million to 265 million people in my lifetime. I constantly tell everyone how great a country it is, and how it provides opportunity to all."

One of America's starkest success stories comes from Depression-era rural Virginia. As a high school student, J.B. Fuqua, now 79, had a plan to be a millionaire by age 30, and this barefoot farm boy raised by his grandparents never looked back. At age 14, he heard an ad for a 25-cent book on how to obtain a ham radio license. He sent in his quarter, received the book, and earned his license. Fuqua, a voracious reader all his life, then discovered that the library at Duke University had a books-by-mail program. He promptly ordered books on commercial radio, earning a license to broadcast as well. Rather than going to college, Fuqua became the youngest radio officer in the U.S. Merchant Marine, and followed that up by becoming the youngest chief engineer of a U.S. commercial radio station.

At the age of 21, with a few years of experience under his belt, the ever-confident Fuqua walked into the Augusta, Georgia, Chamber of Commerce and convinced the executive director to furnish him with the names of three investors who would lend him $10,000 to launch a new radio station. As soon as he had it set up, Fuqua set his sights higher. He couldn't help but notice that "all the big houses were owned by bankers"; so he started ordering books on banking and finance from the Duke mail library and studied them at night. By age 30, he bought a Royal Crown Cola bottling company. And while others were still hesitant to invest in a new industry called television, Fuqua rushed in head first, launching WGAC in Augusta for $250,000. He eventually sold it for $30 million.

Fuqua began buying troubled companies and selling their assets, slowly building the conglomerate now known as Fuqua Industries. In the late 1960s, Fuqua converted the company from a private into a public corporation, and it hit the *Fortune* 500 in just four years.

Asked about his success, Fuqua replies, "There are three Cs to individual achievement: capacity, capital, and courage. And without courage, even if you have the capacity and all the capital in the world to run a business, you won't succeed." Although Fuqua would have liked to have had more formal education, he always felt "prepared for the next step." He thinks today that "there is more opportunity in America than ever before," and notes that "it's now easier to get capital, because there is simply more of it around."

Rather than waiting for books to arrive in the mail from the Duke Library, the semi-retired Fuqua now spends up to two-and-a-half hours a day on the Internet. Technology, he notes, gives today's youngsters a tremendous advantage: they can sit at home and be "in the middle of the largest lending library in the entire world, surrounded by books, magazines, and all kinds of publications."

For his own part, Fuqua remains eternally grateful to Duke. In the 1970s he awarded the school the then-unheard-of sum of $10 million to start the business school that now bears his name. Duke presented him with a gift of their own: the manual on how to obtain a commercial radio license that he had borrowed to get his start over three decades earlier.

THE AMERICAN DREAM IS NOT DEAD

So the next time you hear somebody—probably a politician—trying to pit rich and poor against one another, or claiming that our economic system is closed to little guys, or mourning that the American dream is dead, just remember shoeless J. B. Fuqua, the immigrant Charlie Chea, or Ed Rensi slinging burgers. They faced high odds, but overcame them with optimism and determination, creating opportunities for themselves and others in the process. There is no sign whatsoever that this historic pattern of mobility is letting up. The only foreseeable threat for the future is that our government will so clog America's commercial arteries as to make forward motion of all sorts difficult.

For those who have the energy and dedication, America still operates, like Lincoln declared, as a "just, generous, and prosperous system, which opens the way for all." Reports of Horatio Alger's death are greatly exaggerated.

> "Current wage levels lie significantly
> below the level called for by actual
> worker productivity."

INCREASING THE MINIMUM WAGE
CAN HELP THE WORKING POOR

John McDermott

In 1996, Congress approved an increase in the minimum wage, from $4.25 to $5.15 per hour. In the following viewpoint, written in 1995, John McDermott argues in favor of that wage hike. He contends that an increase in the minimum wage would increase employment and could help raise the bottom quarter of the workforce above the poverty line. However, McDermott asserts, the minimum wage can only be truly effective if it is large enough for families to live on comfortably. McDermott is an editor of *Socialism and Democracy* and the author of *Corporate Society*.

As you read, consider the following questions:

1. What is the "ripple" effect of increasing the minimum wage, according to McDermott?
2. In the author's view, what is one harmful effect of the current wage structure?
3. According to the National Welfare Rights Organization, as cited by the author, how much should the minimum wage be?

Reprinted, by permission, from John McDermott, "Bare Minimum: A Too-Low Minimum Wage Keeps All Wages Down," *Dollars and Sense*, July/August 1995. *Dollars and Sense* is a progressive economics magazine published six times a year. First-year subscriptions cost $18.95 and may be ordered by writing to *Dollars and Sense*, One Summer St., Somerville, MA 02143.

Traditional economic theory and its partisans take the position that increasing the minimum wage must cause unemployment because it "artificially" inflates wages. It's a simple argument: Employees normally produce just about enough to offset their own wages. A higher minimum wage means that some workers won't produce enough to justify their higher wages, and will therefore have to be fired. In the jargon of professional economists, it makes some workers' wages higher than is justified by their "marginal revenue product" (what they contribute to the firm's output).

MINIMUM WAGE AND EMPLOYMENT

But a study by Princeton economists David Card and Alan Krueger plays havoc with this analysis. They show that recent rises in state and federal minimum wages led to increases, not decreases, in the number of workers employed. The Princeton authors call this pattern very, very "robust": it holds up under a wide variety of circumstances, places and times.

There is a striking difference between what traditional economic theory calls for and what actually happens when the minimum wage goes up. In that theory, a minimum wage increase should eliminate jobs—those whose productivity falls below the new, higher productivity standard forced by the wage rise. In fact, however, minimum wage increases expand employment.

In New Jersey, for example, a large increase in the state minimum wage in 1992—an 80 cent rise on a $4.25 base, or almost 19%—was followed by an increase in minimum wage employment at the higher rate. Meanwhile, in neighboring Pennsylvania, which didn't enact a higher rate, minimum wage employment lagged behind that of New Jersey. Similar patterns emerged when the California minimum wage was boosted in 1988, and when the national minimum rose in 1990 and 1991.

This experience doesn't fit conventional wage theory at all, according to which a minimum wage rise should simply lop off the lower edge of jobs. In fact, however, low-wage workers are not fired but are "swept up" to the new minimum. The rise also has a "ripple" effect—workers who earn more than the minimum also get raises as employers try to maintain a structure of wage differentials among different groups and kinds of employees. Then too, employers tend to raise the wages of workers who are not even covered by the federal minimum wage, such as those not engaged in interstate commerce.

This evidence argues that current wage levels lie significantly below the level called for by actual worker productivity. In fact there is much evidence that the minimum wage of recent years has been artificially low. In 1989 the Bush administration insisted on a sub-minimum or training wage for teen-age workers. Pretending not to notice that teen-agers often have to switch jobs from term to term, the Bushites insisted that employers could pay teen-agers a "training wage" 15% less than the existing minimum for up to 180 days. Lobbyists insisted this was a life or death proposition for the industries affected. But the provision was so little used that it was dropped without fanfare in 1993.

The fact is that minimum wage employers find it hard to get workers at the regular rate, much less the cut-price Bush insisted on. Many pay premiums to their employees for bringing in new hires. Often too they voluntarily exceed the legal minimum in order to recruit the workers they need. Thus, a McDonald's in a metropolitan area may start workers at $5.25 or even $5.75 or more per hour, whereas they stick with the legal minimum in, say, Jesse Helm's North Carolina or Newt Gingrich's Georgia.

Card and Krueger seize upon such evidence to argue that conventional wage theory is merely "incomplete." Employers will pay a relatively premium wage so as to recruit all the workers they need and, especially, to stabilize the workforce at a higher level of output performance.

Implicit in this argument, however, is that prior to the minimum wage hikes they were paying less than the output ("marginal revenue product") of their workers justified, and in fact have some leeway in relating their employees' wages to their productivity. This is a crucial point for the current debate since it suggests that much of the wage structure, at least at the lower end, is economically arbitrary. Unfortunately, this very point, and its social consequences, tends to be muted in current discussions of the wage structure.

If anything good is to come out of the debate over the federal minimum, we have to go beyond the narrow issue that increases "might" increase unemployment. It's good to know that they probably won't. But the increases or decreases in unemployment involved are trivial next to the effects of a Federal Reserve Bank policy now calculated to keep unemployment high and workers' pay low. The headline issue of "teen-age unemployment," then, is a hoax. The real issue about the federal minimum wage concerns its wider impact on the thirty-odd million people in the lower quarter of the workforce. Since this is not well-understood we should step back a moment and look into it.

When the minimum wage was first introduced in 1938 it was intended to be only a *transitional* wage, not a *living* wage. It was part of a package of "floors" intended to tide workers over the ebb and flow of the business cycle or season. Like Unemployment Insurance and welfare, the minimum wage was intended to underwrite the period between decent jobs or during dead seasons. Nobody was intended to live on it (though non-metropolitan, particularly southern workers often had to). The idea was that a minimum wage job would tide you over until you landed a "real job" at a living wage, or got a call-back to your regular job.

Because of this transitional character, the level of the minimum wage didn't much affect the wage structure of (metropolitan) industry. That was a matter, mainly, of unions and the secondary pressures that union settlements would generate on non-union employers.

But nowadays, the federal minimum wage has an entirely different significance. One in four workers is a part-timer or a "temp" or some other variety of so-called "contingent" worker, and the unions are in shock. The federal minimum exerts a powerful effect on the wage structure for such workers.

THE "RIPPLE" EFFECT

For example, an increase to $5.75 per hour would directly affect not only the five million workers who receive the present $4.25 minimum, but also at least 15 million others whose present wages fall between $4.25 and $5.75. Moreover, employers maintain a definite structure of wage differentials among their employees. Thus a "ripple" effect occurs as employers adjust upward the pay of higher-level employees so as to maintain the pay structure.

In other words, such an increase will help out virtually all of the 30-odd million workers who make up the lowest quarter of the workforce. Thus, we have to reconceive the minimum wage: it's no longer a transitional wage but is instead a living wage for millions of workers, year in and year out, and a major influence on the living wage levels for a quarter of the workforce.

This is no longer a peripheral economic issue. Several industries rest on the very low wage workforce. These include restaurants, retailers, and nondurable goods manufacturers, particularly in food processing and the needle trades. The National Restaurant Association and a host of other industrial lobbyists spend large sums to keep the minimum wage low. This pressure and money lies behind the ability of anti-minimum wage forces to filibuster proposed increases (1988) and to sustain presidential vetoes when Congress has managed to pass a big increase

(1989). In short, because the federal minimum affects living wages for so many workers, it has become a central economic and political issue.

All this points to a more far-reaching conclusion than the terms of the conventional minimum wage/unemployment debate suggest. I would argue that the very low federal rate of recent years has acted as a wage depressant. What once was intended to push workers' wages up, now seems to press them down.

The sensitivity of so many different wages to the federal minimum shows that employers use the federal rate as a keying wage for their wage and salary structure. When the federal rate goes up, their wages go up across the board. And when the federal rate is stabilized at an artificially low level, it supports the existing, too low wage rates, rates that under-represent workers' real productivity. Thus, the low wage industries, their industrial associations and their supporters in Congress have reversed the effect that minimum wage legislation was originally intended to have. By maintaining the federal minimum so low, the industries have been able to use the minimum to keep wages for vast numbers of other workers down to economically artificial and socially harmful levels.

Four Benefits of the Minimum Wage

As good public policy, the minimum wage has at least four things going for it. First and foremost, it is a way to increase workers' earnings without placing any burden on the taxpayer. It does not add a penny to the federal deficit. If anything, it decreases the deficit by boosting income tax revenue and reducing welfare payments. Second, it provides increased income to workers who do not qualify for government transfer programs or tax credits. Third, it is an incentive to work in the "above ground" economy rather than in the "underground" economy where wages are often higher than the federal minimum. Fourth, and by no means least, an increased minimum wage may well lead to higher productivity in the economy. At current wage levels, there is little incentive for low-wage employers to introduce new technology or find other ways to boost the output of their workforce. Required to pay a higher wage, firms would have an incentive to find ways to use their workers more effectively.

Barry Bluestone and Teresa Ghilarducci, *American Prospect*, May/June 1996.

Among the many harmful effects of the present wage structure is that its lower end has to be subsidized by others. If the employer doesn't pay a living wage, someone else has to make up the difference. Low wage workers typically receive subsidies out of the public treasury in the form of food stamps, welfare, reverse income tax (Earned Income Tax Credit, or EITC), federal and other housing assistance and heating subsidies, Medicaid, school lunch and other programs for children, and so forth. . . .

But, like the old minimum wage, these assistance programs were never designed to provide a long-term income source to such large numbers of people. Thus, when the working poor are added to the poor who cannot find jobs, government social service and related budgets become swamped, and the tax system stressed. The results are all too predictable: too little money for too many people, and the ever present hazard of taxpayer revolt which will cut the available funds even further.

It's hard to calculate the entire weight of this burden on the public treasury, but the following elementary arithmetic tells the important story. The poverty-level income for a family of four is $14,800 per year. Many of these families have one or more family members working. Card and Krueger point out that 36% of minimum wage earners are their family's sole wage earner, and that on average minimum wage earners account for one-half of their families' income. If a hypothetical family of four had the equivalent of one and a half wage earners each making the federal minimum (not an unusual circumstance), that would generate under $13,500 (52 weeks * 60 hours * $4.25 = $13,260). Just to reach the poverty line, someone else has to provide them with about $1,500 per year. At present, that extra $1,500 comes out of the public treasury.

AN UNPREPARED WORKFORCE

These numbers reflect a socially dysfunctional economy. Thirty million workers and their families are at, below, or just above the poverty line. By realistic estimates there are another 12 to 14 million unemployed. In total, nearly a third of the working and potentially working population are maintained at or just above poverty levels only by grace of assistance from the public treasury.

Beyond the dollar costs to the treasury, systematic underpayment of the workforce implies under-investment in present and future workers. This under-investment is confirmed, for example, in the Carnegie Foundation's report on children, released in April 1994, which the New York Times characterized as painting ". . . a bleak picture of disintegrating families, persistent poverty, high levels of child abuse, inadequate health care, and child care of such poor quality that it threatens youngsters' intellectual and emotional development."

It is confirmed in Fordham University's Index of Social Health, which revealed in October 1994 that a composite measure of the U.S. population's overall health fell from 73.8 in 1970 to only 40.6 in 1992. And it is confirmed in the [former] Labor Secretary Robert Reich's pre-occupation with an under-trained and under-prepared actual and potential workforce.

In short, the lower part of the labor force is not paid enough to maintain itself and its current level of skills, much less expand its productive capacities. Nor can workers afford to bring up and educate their children. When a private sector firm makes dresses or processes chickens, for example, it must pay the full production costs of its raw materials, technology, machinery, energy, buildings and so forth. But too many of these firms in too many industries are not paying the full cost of rearing, educating, and maintaining their own workers. They have a parasitic relationship to society and the rest of the economy. They're a drain on the economy, not an asset, a threat to the society, not a contributor.

What would be a realistic minimum wage now? If it were pegged to one-half the average factory wage, as it was intended to be in the first place, the federal minimum would be about $6 per hour. If we were to set it at a family survival level, the inflation in medical, housing and educational costs of recent years would require a rate of $10 or more per hour. The National Welfare Rights Organization has argued that $15/hour would more nearly reflect the real costs of living and the rising costs of raising children who can function in the modern economy.

Would figures like that exceed the ability of employers to pay? We don't know because employer cost structures are "proprietary information" and thus excluded from public view. But the public has a pressing right to know these things because we are paying the bill for the low-wage economy, directly in the tax system and indirectly in the long-range costs of a workforce whose lower levels receive chronically inadequate investment.

These things suggest the terms of a realistic economic debate over the minimum wage: a living, sustainable wage for every worker? Open up industry's books on wage costs? Should low-wage employers be required to underwrite serious technological and/or commercial training for their workers? And, more basic, what are the macroeconomic limits that should be imposed on subsidizing the low-wage economy? How do we move on to higher levels of investment in the labor force? Issues like this won't pass muster in Congress, but President Bill Clinton's administration should be under public pressure to respond to them.

| "Raising the minimum wage may reduce poverty slightly for workers who keep their jobs, but it will do nothing for the vast majority of the poor who do not work."

INCREASING THE MINIMUM WAGE IS COUNTERPRODUCTIVE

Mark Wilson

In the following viewpoint, Mark Wilson argues against the minimum wage increase proposed by President Bill Clinton in 1995 (Congress approved the proposal, which raised the minimum wage to $5.15 per hour, in 1996). Wilson contends that increasing the wage will cause a reduction of entry-level job opportunities. In addition, Wilson maintains, an increase in the minimum wage will not reduce poverty because most minimum wage workers are not their families' primary earners. Instead, he asserts, alternatives to a minimum wage hike—such as education and tax reforms—would better assist the poor. Wilson is the Rebecca Lukens Fellow in Labor Policy for the Heritage Foundation, a conservative public policy research foundation.

As you read, consider the following questions:

1. In what three ways do firms respond to higher labor costs, according to Wilson?
2. According to the author, how many new minimum wage job opportunities could be created in lieu of a wage increase?
3. In the author's view, how does the capital gains tax affect wages?

Reprinted from Mark Wilson, "Why Raising Minimum Wage Is a Bad Idea," *Backgrounder*, May 17, 1995, by permission of The Heritage Foundation.

R aising the minimum wage, like mandating universal health insurance coverage, does not come without cost. The question is: Where are the costs incurred, and do they outweight the benefits? . . .

THE IMPACT OF AN INCREASED MINIMUM WAGE

Even though a few recent studies disagree on the employment effects of increasing the minimum wage, most economists do agree on several key points.

• Raising the minimum wage will reduce entry-level job opportunities, particularly for low-skilled Americans. Some of the entry-level jobs that would be created in a growing economy will not be created.

• There may be a labor supply effect that results in a measured increase in total employment, but labor demand certainly will be altered. Americans may apply for minimum wage jobs in greater numbers, but employers will hire only the most skilled among them.

• Raising the minimum wage may reduce poverty slightly for workers who keep their jobs, but it will do nothing for the vast majority of poor who do not work.

• Employers will raise prices for the poor and non-poor alike to offset increased labor costs.

Factors operating interactively on both the demand and supply sides of the labor market will determine the magnitude and incidence of any effects of increasing the minimum wage. The magnitude also will be affected by the growth rate of the economy at the time. In a growing economy with significant gains in productivity, increases in the minimum wage can be absorbed by some firms without necessarily decreasing employment. However, as President George Bush discovered, raising the minimum wage during a recession can place a significant brake on employment growth—which probably contributed to his now infamous "job-less" recovery.

THE RESPONSE OF FIRMS

Increases in the minimum wage do affect a firm's employment, prices, and profits, although the pattern of these effects will vary from company to company. Studies indicate that firms facing higher labor costs, and therefore a change in the relative costs of labor and capital, respond in up to three ways, all of which hurt Americans.

1. *Firms may raise prices.*

If an increase in the minimum wage is phased in during a period of above-average inflation, employers may find it easier to pass increased labor costs on to consumers. However, in periods of relative price stability, employers may not have this option (at least to the same degree) and will seek instead to cut other production or sales costs. Firms facing stagnant demand for their goods and services and not readily able to adjust their production and sales costs will have little choice but to raise prices or cut profits. Economic models of the U.S. economy indicate that even a 75 cent increase in the minimum wage over three years adds 0.2 percentage points to the Consumer Price Index.

2. *Firms may reduce or eliminate pay raises, bonuses, or benefits for their other employees or reduce other costs.*

Besides reducing compensation for non-minimum wage workers, firms may try to negotiate lower prices from their suppliers. They also may take steps to increase productivity by reducing the rate of new hiring and postponing the replacement of employees who quit, by reducing working hours (particularly for unskilled workers), or by replacing lower skilled workers with higher skilled workers as low-skilled workers quit. Employers also will likely try to replace some workers with machines.

3. *Firms may accept lower profits in the short run.*

Some lawmakers contend that an increase in the minimum wage could be accommodated easily without layoffs or price rises because profits are up. But profits, as a share of the Gross Domestic Product (GDP), have only just returned to their long-run average level after a ten-year period of below-average profits, and many industries are still reporting mixed profit results. And, of course, industries with generally low profit margins in any case will have a hard time finding the earnings to pay for an increase in the minimum wage.

POTENTIAL JOB LOSSES

Estimates of the disemployment effect of raising the minimum wage can be done in a number of ways. Different job loss numbers are derived, for instance, when considering different employment groups or using different methodologies. Focusing only on teenagers, and using the average disemployment effects found in David Card and Alan Krueger, suggests a job loss estimate for teens of 51,000 to 99,000. If one considers both teenagers and young adults (ages 16 to 24), raising the minimum wage to $5.15 would result in about 508,000 to 677,000 jobs lost for this group of workers, according to a study by David Neumark and William Wascher. A macroeconomic computer model of the U.S. economy indicates that increasing the minimum wage will result in creation of 400,000 fewer jobs by the year 2000.

Another way to estimate the number of lost entry-level job opportunities would be to calculate the total cost of the increase in labor costs from raising the minimum wage and then to divide that total by the average cost of an existing minimum wage worker. A 97 cents per hour rise (mandated increase plus employer-paid Federal Insurance Contributions Act [FICA] and Federal Unemployment Tax Act [FUTA] taxes) in the minimum wage times 25 hours per week, times 38 weeks per year, times 2.738 million minimum wage workers equals a $2.191 billion increase in labor costs for employers. This $2.2 billion increase in labor costs is roughly what employers would need to create 576,000 new minimum wage job opportunities for low-skilled workers at $4.25 per hour.

It also is important to note that the effect of increasing the minimum wage may be influenced by other legislation and regulatory actions that affect the relative cost of labor and capital. Federally mandated benefits and Occupational Safety and Health Administration (OSHA)-proposed regulations, such as ergonomics, interact with a higher minimum wage to increase the cost of labor relative to capital. Combined, these could permanently reduce the demand for low-skilled, low-wage entry-level jobs as employers substitute capital and other efficiencies in sales and production for labor hours.

FAULTY PREMISES

Aside from the costs associated with raising the minimum wage, proponents present an emotionally appealing case. However, close economic analysis reveals that their premises are faulty. Examples:

• *Since 1983, the historic value of work has not declined.* In fact, the real value of total compensation—wages plus fringe benefits—has increased. From 1983 to 1994, the employment cost index for wages and salaries increased an average of 3.7 percent per year, and average hourly earnings increased 3.1 percent. To be sure, during that period, inflation averaged 3.7 percent. But fringe benefits have risen more rapidly than earnings, so the employment cost index for *total* compensation per hour increased faster than inflation over the same period (4.2 percent).

Further, there is now widespread consensus that the Consumer Price Index (CPI) significantly overstates the rate of increase in the cost of living. Without the upward bias in the CPI, even real wages would have grown since 1983.

• Raising the minimum wage does not help primarily adult workers who rely on their jobs to support their families. For the most part, the 2.7 million workers who earn the minimum wage can be broken down into two broad groups.

About half are teenagers or young adults aged 21 or less, and most (68.2 percent) live in families with incomes two or more times the official poverty level for their family size. The average family income of a teenage minimum wage worker is around $47,000. Only 12 percent of these young workers live in poor families.

The other half are workers ages 22 and higher. More of these workers live in poor families (27 percent or 367,000 have family incomes below the poverty level) or near poverty (44 percent have family incomes less than one and a half times the poverty level). However, even among this half of the minimum wage population, 39 percent live in families with incomes two or more times the poverty level, and the average family income of minimum wage workers aged 25 to 61 is around $25,000.

THE OVERLAP BETWEEN POVERTY AND MINIMUM WAGE WORKERS

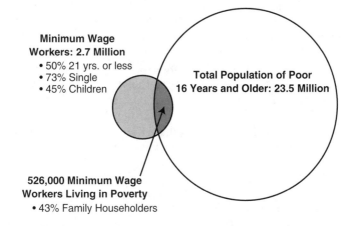

Minimum Wage Workers: 2.7 Million
- 50% 21 yrs. or less
- 73% Single
- 45% Children

Total Population of Poor 16 Years and Older: 23.5 Million

526,000 Minimum Wage Workers Living in Poverty
- 43% Family Householders

Source: Heritage Foundation calculations from the Census Bureau's March 1993 *Annual Demographic File.*

Contrary to [former] Labor Secretary Robert Reich's claim that a 90 cent increase in the minimum wage will not cost any jobs, a recent study indicates that a similar increase in 1990/91 caused a significant employment loss for both groups. According to the study, which was conducted by Finis Welch of Texas

A&M University and others, employment declined by 7.3 percent and 11.4 percent for teenage men and women, and 3.1 percent and 5.2 percent for adult high school dropouts.

• *Minimum wage workers for the most part are secondary earners in their families, not the primary earners.*

Only 23 percent of minimum wage workers were the sole breadwinners in their families in the previous year. The wage and salary earnings of 56 percent of minimum wage workers account for 25 percent or less of their families' total wage and salary incomes.

Only 16 percent of minimum wage workers are full-year/full-time employees. Thirty-three percent are part-year/part-time employees, and almost half (48.5 percent) are voluntary part-time workers.

Almost 40 percent of the sole breadwinners earning the minimum wage are voluntary part-time workers, while only 18.8 percent of all minimum wage workers are family heads or spouses working full-time.

ALTERNATIVES TO RAISING THE MINIMUM WAGE

Contrary to assertions by practitioners of class warfare, employers do not—indeed cannot—unfairly keep down the wages of their lower-skilled and entry-level employees. Employers, as well as employees, operate within a competitive labor market in which wage rates broadly reflect the productivity of workers— less the costs of government-imposed mandates and taxes associated with employing a worker. Raising prices and destroying entry-level job opportunities is not the sensible way to increase real wages. Instead of raising the minimum wage, Congress and the Administration should focus on policies that will increase wages and job opportunities for Americans by improving labor productivity and reducing the cost of employing workers. Specifically:

• *To the extent that government continues to set minimum wages, responsibility for setting minimum wage levels and enforcing the other provisions of the Fair Labor Standards Act (FLSA) should be turned over to the states.*

Minimum wage laws presume that politicians are morally justified in destroying some people's jobs in order to inflate other people's wages. The current minimum wage effectively prohibits people from working unless their labor is worth at least $4.25 [$5.15 as of 1997] an hour. On this basis alone, the minimum wage should be abolished. However, if there is a minimum wage, it should at least reflect the real labor cost and market differences in different regions of the country. . . .

Abolishing the federal minimum wage would allow governors and state legislators to determine the minimums for their own states if they believe such action to be helpful. This would allow proponents to set minimum wages according to local labor market conditions and living costs while taking into account how business and employment conditions would be affected. Having a national minimum wage makes as much sense as requiring the federal government to pay the same wage for entry-level jobs in New York City and Fargo, North Dakota.

REFORMS ARE NEEDED

• *Enact significant regulatory reform.*

The explosion of new regulations since 1988 has raised the cost of labor and capital, created barriers to the formation of new companies and jobs, and raised the cost of employing Americans. This higher cost of employment in turn means that, in a competitive economy, the return to labor in the form of wages is reduced. Some government regulation is desirable and necessary, but the plethora of new regulations has placed a significant burden on businesses' ability to create jobs for unskilled workers. This burden needs to be rolled back, not only to allow wages to rise, but also to decrease the cost of hiring workers. . . .

• *Promote education reforms that will raise the skills and productivity of entry-level workers.*

Employers cannot pay wages that exceed the revenue generated by a worker—at least not if they intend to stay in business. Thus, one way to raise wages without job losses and other costs is to raise the skills and productivity of workers, especially entry-level workers, through radical reform of the nation's schools.

Despite record spending of taxpayers' dollars, America's public schools continue to turn out far too many high school graduates who lack not only basic skills, but also the communication skills and work attitudes that employers need. This depresses the wages these workers can earn. It is not unreasonable for employers to expect that after 12 years of schooling individuals should have a reasonable competence in basic core skills (verbal communication, reading, writing, arithmetic, and basic sciences). Public schools routinely fail to prepare people for work, and then government minimum wage laws prohibit them from working.

A strong core curriculum should be taught in all high schools, and real testing should be instituted to indicate to parents whether or not their children's schools are achieving acceptable standards. School choice legislation is needed to give schools the financial incentive to respond to demands by parents that they meet these standards.

• *Reduce the Capital Gains Tax.*

The United States taxes corporate income twice: first at the corporate level, then at the personal level. Recognizing this, many other industrial nations have eliminated or reduced the taxation of these gains. The capital gains tax affects wages because it reduces capital spending, technological innovation, and new ventures. This hurts labor productivity and wages in the long run.

Although reducing capital gains taxes is portrayed by the practitioners of class warfare as benefiting only the rich, the benefits flow to all workers. Well over half of all taxpayers with capital gains in 1992 had adjusted gross incomes of less than $50,000. Over 73 percent had incomes of less than $75,000.

Often overlooked benefits include:

• On average, wage earners receive $12 after taxes for every $1 of after-tax income received by investors. More than 90 percent of the benefits of new investment would flow to wage earners, not to owners of capital.

• Past reductions in the capital gains tax rate (1978 and 1981) stimulated the start-up of new businesses and the expansion of job opportunities.

• A lower capital gains tax would raise the expected rate of return on investment in the U.S. and provide an incentive for both American and foreign firms to put their capital to work here with American workers. . . .

THE PATH CONGRESS SHOULD TAKE

Raising the minimum wage appeals to the American sense of decency and compassion. But it would be a mistake. Raising the minimum wage would impose significant costs, primarily on those unskilled Americans a minimum wage hike is supposed to help. It also would raise prices for both the poor and non-poor. It would destroy entry-level job opportunities that otherwise would have been created; and although it could raise some workers' family incomes above poverty, it would do so at the cost of denying jobs to many more.

To raise the standard of living of minimum wage workers without imposing these costs, Congress should focus on policies that raise worker productivity while reducing government-imposed labor costs on employers.

"If we are going to invest money...
to help poor families, it makes sense
to invest it in ways that will help
them enter the workforce and
become self-sufficient."

WELFARE-TO-WORK PROGRAMS ARE EFFECTIVE

Tommy Thompson

In the wake of welfare reform legislation passed in 1996, states are devising programs to move people from welfare to work. In the following viewpoint, Tommy Thompson, the Republican governor of Wisconsin, describes his state's welfare-to-work system, which he believes can serve as a model for other states. Wisconsin's programs have helped welfare recipients develop a work ethic and find employment, Thompson argues. He contends that people on welfare want to work, but they need resources such as child care and transportation in order to obtain jobs. Programs that provide these resources and require recipients to work for their welfare payments instill a work ethic and make participants more employable, Thompson claims.

As you read, consider the following questions:
1. According to Thompson, what is illogical about Aid to Families with Dependent Children?
2. How would Thompson change the health care system?
3. By what percentage has Wisconsin reduced its welfare caseload, according to the author?

Reprinted from Tommy Thompson, "The Good News About Welfare Reform: Wisconsin's Success Story," *The Heritage Lectures*, No. 593, August 11, 1997, with permission of The Heritage Foundation.

During the past two years, governors like myself have spent quite a bit of time in Washington trying to persuade Congress to give them the flexibility and the opportunity to design and operate their own welfare reform programs. We are thankful that Congress finally heeded our calls to end the old dysfunctional welfare system and to entrust the states with designing appropriate replacement programs.

Now, as states begin to structure these programs, they are looking for good ideas. What is working elsewhere? What kinds of programs are on the cutting edge? I appreciate the fact that Heritage Senior Policy Analyst Robert Rector singled out Wisconsin as a strong model for other states in his article in *Policy Review*, not just because of our successes in reforming welfare, but because of our vast experience in trying different methods. But success, it has been said, has a thousand parents. That's why President Bill Clinton has even tried to claim credit for Wisconsin's welfare reform (although he would not give us the waivers we needed).

Long before it was popular to talk about reforming welfare, Wisconsin has been constantly reforming its welfare program over the last decade. The state successfully constructed a whole new system to eliminate welfare. In fact, we officially stopped "welfare" as you know it in September 1997. No other state can come close to matching that experience.

Helping Welfare Recipients Work

Welfare reform in Wisconsin began with one simple premise: Every person is capable of doing something. The challenge for government is to help people go from doing nothing to doing something. If we are going to invest money as a society or as a state to help poor families, it makes sense to invest it in ways that will help them enter the workforce and become self-sufficient—instead of sending checks out once a month and in effect just walking away from their needs. To me, the latter is not compassion. Expecting nothing in return and offering no real help is hardly compassionate. That is apathy.

When we first started working on reforming welfare in Wisconsin, I invited individual mothers on welfare to visit the executive residence. You can imagine how somebody from a poor neighborhood might feel being invited to the governor's mansion in Madison and sitting down with the governor to talk about personal problems. I do this on a regular basis because I enjoy inviting them to the executive residence for lunch. Why? I wanted to know straight from those who were on welfare why they were on welfare.

We found their answers to be very simple, yet very profound. They wanted to work—something I always had believed was the case—but they were concerned about being unable to afford health care for their children, to obtain quality child care, and to find transportation to and from their jobs. They could not afford to pay for these necessities on their own, especially for health care. So they stayed on welfare as a means to care for their families.

From these meetings and from related research, we began to understand how government could help these families become self-sufficient. The solution was not simply to hand them a check to cash and walk away. The solution was developing meaningful programs that could support them in their struggle for independence—programs for child care, health care, job search assistance, and transportation. The solution was to provide these programs as a ladder to help them climb out of poverty and off welfare. So we immediately started shifting resources to these areas.

THE LADDER OF OPPORTUNITY

The next step we took was obvious yet unprecedented: We began to expect something in return from the people we were helping, not the least of which was evidence that they were taking on personal responsibility for their own improvement and for their families. Wisconsin was going to expect the people it helped to get up in the morning and go to work! It was a radical notion: Get up in the morning, get the kids ready for school or child care, go to work on time, earn a paycheck, and support your family—ultimately without any reliance on the government for help. If Wisconsin was going to offer them a ladder, then we would require them to use the ladder.

These simple principles formed the foundation for all of Wisconsin's welfare reforms over the past decade. And they serve as the foundation of the new "W2" program, Wisconsin's replacement for the old welfare system, that will be in place shortly.

Perhaps the greatest lesson America has learned from the failed welfare system is that giving something for nothing does not work. Welfare does not help a person lead a better life, and it does not help a person get out of poverty. As we worked to reform the welfare system in Wisconsin, we found that we could not rely on hoping to find any "silver bullets." There weren't any. So we set in motion a series of innovative programs based on very basic principles. . . .

Work First. Incredibly, the welfare system actually penalized two young parents, especially teenagers, if they got married and both had jobs. If you got married, you couldn't receive welfare, but whether you lived together or apart, if you did not get married, you could receive Aid to Families with Dependent Children (AFDC). If a young mother stayed single, she could get welfare, but if she married the father of her child, they wouldn't receive AFDC even if the husband didn't have any work experience. It was illogical. Naturally, they would choose to stay apart, so their families did not become self-sufficient. To this day, I cannot understand that approach at all. So we looked for ways to change it.

WORKFARE TEACHES RESPONSIBILITY

Aside from their benefit checks, workfare participants gain something else. They learn skills and the sense of responsibility necessary for moving from welfare to work permanently. For people on welfare, who have a hard time getting their feet in an employer's door, workfare at least gives them a fighting chance to compete later on.

Robert A. Sirico, *New York Times*, July 27, 1997.

We designed Work First specifically to address this problem. Work First steered welfare applicants into jobs instead of onto welfare. It provided job search assistance and even personal financial planning. There are a lot of people who just need basic help with their personal finances or finding a job and staying afloat. Work First tried to provide that help up front by providing options to welfare. This program has removed the disincentives in the welfare system that discouraged young couples from marrying and both working.

Work, Not Welfare. The next program we instituted is the prelude to W2. This program, which we piloted in two counties in Wisconsin, required participants to find a job within 24 months or lose their welfare benefits. In fact, when we started Work, Not Welfare, such a program had not even been talked about in Washington, D.C. It was the first program that absolutely required welfare recipients to find work—the first program that put into practice the philosophy that welfare was a temporary program, not a way of life.

INSTILLING A WORK ETHIC

Pay for Performance and Self Sufficiency First. We followed Work, Not Welfare with Pay for Performance and Self Sufficiency First. A lot of people only need food stamps to make ends meet, but we were finding that quite often when these people went to apply for food stamps, they ended up being handled in Social Services, where they were told they had to sign up for AFDC as well. Many of these people didn't want AFDC, but once they started receiving it, they stayed in the program, and nobody expected anything else from them. We knew this had to change.

Our work-based programs, Pay for Performance and Self Sufficiency First, are forerunners to Wisconsin's new W2 program. These work-based programs replicate real-world working situations, and they place an emphasis on self sufficiency. First, we targeted those applying for welfare and put them on Pay for Performance; then we targeted those already on welfare.

Both programs are based on very simple, basic, yet fundamental principles. In order to receive an AFDC check, a person must perform certain duties. For example, a person now must be enrolled in our jobs program and spend a minimum of 20 hours a week looking for a job, performing a community service activity, or improving basic skills like résumé writing and interviewing. If he does not perform his prescribed duties, he will not get paid—just like in the real world. If he participates 16 hours a week instead of 20, he will get paid for 16 hours, and his AFDC checks are reduced by 4 hours. If he does not participate at all, he will not get an AFDC check.

HEALTH CARE FOR THE POOR

These programs are straightforward: you work for your check, and your check reflects the amount of work you do in a week— again, just like in the real world. We still provide our participants with ample child care, health care, and transportation, so there are no excuses not to go to work. The goal of Pay for Performance and Self Sufficiency First is to increase the employability of the participants as well as to instill in them a real-world work ethic.

Let me add a word about health care: We have invested a lot of money in supporting a mother who is working with adequate health care for her children. We subsidize them an extra 12 months over the 3 months that AFDC gives them until they are on their feet and able to buy into a health care program on their own. We have a very successful medical assistance program in Wisconsin, and I asked President Bill Clinton for a waiver to allow the working poor just above the poverty line to buy into this program, too, so that they could have the same kind of medical coverage. It would have made so much sense. Low wage earners would pay for part of this assistance, and the state would subsidize the rest, and together we could do a much better job. I think this could become a model for the country and it would help cover a lot more children that don't have health care today. But the President, this President, turned me down. Eventually, I will get this program in place, but it may take a few more years.

THE PROGRAMS HAVE WORKED

Wisconsin's W2 Program. In the end, we must get people off AFDC and move them into the work force. Pay for Performance is paving the way for W2, our next bold step. W2 removes AFDC and cash handouts entirely from the equation. No one will receive cash from the government of Wisconsin any more. He will receive a paycheck either from a private employer or for a community service job. If he does not work, he will not get paid. It is that simple and that straightforward.

So how has Wisconsin changed under these reforms? More important, how have Wisconsin's families done under our reforms? Over the past decade, we have cut Wisconsin's welfare caseload by 60 percent. That means roughly 55,000 families in Wisconsin no longer are trapped in welfare and a life of poverty. This incredible figure includes significant reductions in the welfare rolls in our largest urban center, Milwaukee, which has experienced a 32 percent reduction.

Families are happier, too, because they are at least $5,000 a year better off financially by working, even at a minimum wage job, than they would be by staying on AFDC. Mothers and fathers have more self-esteem. Their children are doing better socially and in school. And the entire family has a more optimistic outlook. They are pursuing the American dream instead of wallowing in the despair of welfare. . . .

I am equally confident that every state in this country can have similar successes, especially in helping families climb out of poverty. I hope the Wisconsin experience can provide both inspiration and insight as states work to replace the failed welfare system. Abraham Lincoln once said, "You cannot help men permanently by doing for them what they could and should do for themselves." This is a basic principle of good government and a principle behind all of our efforts in Wisconsin. It is why Wisconsin's welfare reforms have worked so well.

| "The arbitrary nature of workfare programs will waste [women's] time and, worse, keep them from the very activities which might prepare them for work."

WELFARE-TO-WORK PROGRAMS HARM THE POOR

Liz Krueger and John E. Seley

Workfare programs, such as the one in New York City, actually undermine effective job searches, argue Liz Krueger and John E. Seley in the following viewpoint. They maintain that these programs make finding viable employment more difficult by placing welfare recipients in low-skill jobs and curtailing efforts to obtain an education. In addition, the authors contend, workfare programs will result in lost jobs and lower wages. Krueger is the associate director of the Community Food Resource Center in New York City. Seley is a professor of urban studies and environmental psychology at the City University of New York.

As you read, consider the following questions:

1. According to Lawrence Mishel and John Schmitt, as cited by the authors, how much income would be lost to low-wage workers throughout the United States in order to accommodate former welfare recipients?
2. According to Krueger and Seley, what is the contradiction of New York City's work requirements?
3. How many workfare-eligible single-adult assistance recipients in New York City found jobs between October 1994 and September 1995, as stated by the authors?

Reprinted, by permission, from Liz Krueger and John E. Seley, "The Return of Slavery: Lessons from Workfare in New York City," *Dollars and Sense*, November/December 1996. *Dollars and Sense* is a progressive economics magazine published six times a year. First-year subscriptions cost $18.95 and may be ordered by writing to *Dollars and Sense*, One Summer St., Somerville, MA 02143.

Many of the provisions of the 1996 "welfare deform" legislation are ill-spirited and cruel. Some are just insulting and bizarre, like the provision to allocate $250 million over five years "to provide education, . . . mentoring, counseling, and adult supervision to promote abstinence from sexual activity. . . ." And the Congress and President Bill Clinton have reserved some of their most irrational demands for an area which might otherwise hold great hope for those struggling to move our of poverty, namely going to work.

Millions of women will be forced into "workfare" assignments—programs requiring welfare recipients to work in exchange for their cash benefits. In the past such jobs had to be in the public or non-profit sectors, unless a state received a waiver to place them with for-profit employers. Under the new law, all employers are eligible.

WORKFARE UNDERMINES WOMEN AND UNIONS

But the laudable objective of moving women into real jobs has been and will be thoroughly undermined. Indeed, rather than get them jobs, the arbitrary nature of workfare programs will waste their time and, worse, keep them from the very activities which might prepare them for work, like schooling and job training.

Worse still, without any real effort at job creation and job preparation, the workfare "employees" will replace existing workers, undermine unions, and further exacerbate the cycle of poverty. They will use up their few years of lifetime eligibility, moving no closer to the stated goal of self-sufficiency, while unwittingly disrupting or displacing low-skilled workers. How do we know? Because New York City has been practicing workfare for several years, and, from 1995 to 1996, almost exactly as the new legislation mandates it.

Why worry about New York? Because New York City's profile of welfare recipients and work is more like the rest of the urban nation than is that of Wisconsin, the dubious success story Republicans like to tout. In New York, we have seen the future and it is not a pretty sight.

There are few jobs and insufficient resources to train people. The New York State Department of Labor declared that New York City would see a maximum of 91,000 job openings in 1996. With a minimum of 750,000 job seekers in the City—520,000 who are on public assistance plus 230,000 "officially" unemployed, and tens of thousands more unofficially unemployed—there will be less than a one-in-eight chance of finding a job.

Addressing the much bigger problem of unemployment would require tens of billions of dollars invested in national job creation strategies.

WAGES WILL FALL

Faced with the frenzied chorus of modern-day know-nothings screaming to "make the poor work," what has New York done? Instead of preparing those in poverty to compete for the few available jobs, it has placed public assistance recipients into unpaid City work assignments with no future. These are not new jobs and they will not move people off welfare. Conveniently, Mayor Rudolph Giuliani has, in the name of fiscal constraint, been able to reduce the city's paid workforce.

Workfare actually shrinks the paid labor market by decreasing paying jobs and wages in the public sector, a traditional route out of poverty in many urban areas. So, while those in the labor market are squeezed from the bottom, those hoping to move off welfare and into the workforce have no place to move but down. Meanwhile, the new lifetime benefit limits are a time-bomb ticking away at each family's financial security. Lose-lose.

To compound the problem of public sector job loss is the slashing of private sector jobs and wages that would occur if former welfare recipients actually did find jobs without displacing current workers. According to Lawrence Mishel and John Schmitt of the Economic Policy Institute, the wages of low-wage workers would have to fall by 11.9% nationally in order to accommodate a million former welfare clients. In New York State, due to the size of its welfare population, wages would have to fall by 17.1%. Mishel and Schmitt say that the net result would be an annual loss of $36 billion in income to low-wage workers throughout the country, or $8.5 billion more than total federal and state spending on Aid to Families with Dependent Children (AFDC) in 1994.

In 1995, Giuliani committed his administration to creating the largest workfare program in the United States. His spokespeople claimed that by late 1997 they would have more than 50,000 single adults and at least 35,000 AFDC mothers in workfare "jobs" (unlike many areas of the country, in New York poor adults without children have been able to receive cash assistance). So there would be over 85,000 welfare participants working off their benefits in government and nonprofit positions. At a hearing in May 1996, the head of the City's Human Resources Administration (the welfare agency) testified that there were already 27,000 single adults in workfare programs.

State legislation required that by January 1997, 90% of the eligible single adult population, or roughly 80,000 people on public assistance, be in workfare assignments. Under the new federal laws, by the year 2005, 200,000 AFDC mothers state-wide will have to take work activities.

NO SKILLS ASSESSMENT

New York City's workfare program has not assessed participants for employability and skill levels prior to giving them workfare assignments and has not trained them for their new "careers." This is equivalent to using a roulette wheel to select employees and place them in jobs. So what is the likelihood that the participants will end up with full-time jobs and careers?

One reason the City does not conduct assessment or training is that it saves a great deal of money. Then, too, the City has no intention of giving workfare recipients assignments which require any specialized skills. Thus, the great majority of the 21,000 workfare placements in New York City as of March 26, 1996, were in "maintenance" positions, primarily at the Parks Department (29% of all workfare placements), the Department of General Services (10%), which takes care of the City's buildings and other facilities, and the Sanitation Department (7%). Sanitation accounts for another 12% in street cleaning activities. The welfare department itself uses 1,300 workfare participants to do clerical work. And the number of workfare participants assigned to each agency are comparable to the layoffs in those agencies.

EDUCATION IS DEVALUED

As more and more public assistance recipients are forced into non-training workfare assignments, other options are undermined and curtailed. For example, although higher education is a proven path to employment and higher wages, the workfare program in New York has forced participants to abandon college in large numbers. Studies show that a community college degree adds $5,000 a year to graduates' incomes, and a bachelor's degree adds an additional $7,000 a year. But since workfare expanded in 1995, the City University of New York (CUNY) reported that 5,000 single adults receiving public assistance were forced to drop out, and another 5,000 to 10,000 welfare mothers were expected to have to quit CUNY by the end of 1996.

In addition, there are 14,000 participants in adult literacy programs in New York City who are in imminent danger of being forced out. Why? Because the workfare assignments are at the same time as classes—no exceptions, no choices, no accommodation. In the City's program, it is preferable to spend twenty-five hours picking up trash in the parks than to get a college degree or other education.

Such punitive work requirements have characterized poverty policy on and off since Colonial times. Nonetheless, they present a contradiction. The lack of assessment and training in New York was a direct violation of federal law, which mandated that participants be provided training appropriate to meet employers' requirements and lead to paid employment. That provision was only removed under the new federal law.

If the regulations for assessment and training were not followed in New York City under the previous mandate, what is the likelihood that they will be provided now that they are no longer required? Beyond New York, even if a locale decides to take a more humane and rational approach, almost all educational and training activities are explicitly prohibited under the new federal legislation.

WORKFARE IS NOT REAL EMPLOYMENT

A workfare participant is not likely to get a permanent job picking up scrap paper in a park if it is designated a "workfare" job with no full-time jobholders. In 1995, only 250 out of 75,000 participants obtained paid jobs in the agencies they were assigned to. Of these, 175 were hired for seasonal work by the Parks Department. Fiscally-strapped communities will only move them into real public sector jobs if unions, the participants and advocacy groups make them.

But while some groups have long been organizing against workfare, others are only starting now. In September 1996, the largest municipal union in New York, the American Federation of State, County and Municipal Employees, asked for a moratorium on workfare, later dropping the demand. The transit workers union called for workfare recipients to be hired into permanent jobs, while also agreeing that more of them can be assigned to clean subways, replacing union employees who have voluntarily left their jobs.

Workfare assignments are not real jobs. Participants cannot work more hours for extra money or comp time, or qualify for a better paying position based on skill or effort. Moreover, under the new federal rules, as participants are required to move from 20 to 30 hours per week in workfare activities over the next six years, their hourly wages will fall. [In the fall of 1997, the New York State Legislature passed a law guaranteeing workfare recipients the minimum wage.]

In the future, welfare recipients will be forced to "work" longer hours, while their opportunities to find a paying job before they use up their family's lifetime assistance limits dwindle away. No matter how well they perform, there are no opportunities for promotion, extra pay, or raises. There is no sick leave. They will receive no pension, and will have little right to refuse assignments even due to specific health and safety conditions.

In a program supposedly designed to turn welfare recipients into motivated employees, there is no motivation for workfare participants to do anything but show up. And not showing up is met with severe sanctions, including the loss of all benefits for months after only one absence. Coupled with the lack of training and skills assessment, this would hardly qualify as a model employment program. Indeed, the slavelike standards forced upon workfare participants have already made it more difficult for unionized City workers to negotiate their own job conditions.

A FAILED EMPLOYMENT PROGRAM

The record of placements verifies the failure of the workfare program as an employment strategy. From October 1994 through September 1995, the City's regular job training program claimed a success rate of 59%. But during the same period, out of 80,000 workfare-eligible single-adult assistance recipients only 5%, or 4,200, found jobs.

For the years just before the workfare-only option was put in effect, the record of movement of single adults from welfare to work was significantly better. For example, from October 1993 to September 1994, 862 people per month moved from welfare to work, compared to 420 monthly the following year.

We have learned during the 1995–1996 experiment with workfare that the government can and will throw its poorest residents off of benefits to avoid costs; it will violate its own obligations to provide quality employment and training programs when faced with no real job opportunities; it will use workfare to displace full-time paid employees; and it will not use workfare to move people into the labor market, private or public.

One analysis estimates that the added costs of workfare will be $10,000 per family of three, including $6,500 for day care and $3,500 for supervisors, transportation, supplies, and administrative costs. This is far greater than the maximum $6,900 public assistance grant provided now to that same family. Like New York, many cities and states may simply find it easier and cheaper to throw people off of welfare, in an unashamed "race to the bottom" of spending on their poor.

PERIODICAL BIBLIOGRAPHY

The following articles have been selected to supplement the diverse views presented in this chapter. Addresses are provided for periodicals not indexed in the *Readers' Guide to Periodical Literature*, the *Alternative Press Index*, the *Social Sciences Index*, or the *Index to Legal Periodicals and Books*.

Robert J. Barro	"Workfare Still Beats Welfare," *Hoover Institution Newsletter*, Summer 1996. Available from the Hoover Institution, Stanford University, Stanford, CA 94305-6010.
Barry Bluestone and Teresa Ghilarducci	"Rewarding Work: Feasible Antipoverty Policy," *American Prospect*, May/June 1996.
Christopher Conte	"Welfare, Work, and the States," *CQ Researcher*, December 6, 1996. Available from 1414 22nd St. NW, Washington, DC 20037.
Neil deMause	"Live Welfare Free or Die," *Z Magazine*, April 1995.
Jason DeParle	"Welfare Law Weighs Heavily on Delta, Where Jobs Are Few," *New York Times*, October 16, 1997.
John Greenwald	"Off the Dole and On the Job," *Time*, August 18, 1997.
John Harwood	"The Bumpy Road from Welfare to Work," *Wall Street Journal*, May 15, 1997.
Bob Herbert	"Many Inner-City Jobs Have No Way Up," *Liberal Opinion*, December 11, 1995. Available from 108 E. Fifth St., Vinton, IA 52349.
Peter T. Kilborn	"Jobs, but Few New Skills, for Those on Welfare," *New York Times*, May 12, 1997.
Norman Ornstein	"Can America Afford a Minimum-Wage Increase?" *Washington Post National Weekly Edition*, February 20–26, 1995. Available from 1150 15th St. NW, Washington, DC 20071.
Kurt L. Schmoke	"Welfare Reform: A Work in Progress," *Vital Speeches of the Day*, November 15, 1997.
Mark Skousen	"Why Wages Rise," *Freeman*, August 1996. Available from the Foundation for Economic Education, 30 S. Broadway, Irvington-on-Hudson, NY 10533.
James L. Tyson	"Pioneer Plan Gets Folks Off Welfare," *Christian Science Monitor*, April 12, 1995.
Andrew White	"WEP: (Workers Expect Paychecks)," *City Limits*, March 1997.

CHAPTER 4

HOW CAN POOR PEOPLE BE HELPED?

CHAPTER PREFACE

The responsibility of helping America's poor has fallen largely on the government since President Franklin Delano Roosevelt initiated his New Deal programs during the Great Depression. However, in recent years many people have debated whether private charities, especially religious organizations, are better equipped to aid the poor.

Some argue that private charity organizations can better serve the poor because they can provide more individualized services than a vast government bureaucracy can. In addition, charity proponents maintain, religious groups can offer spiritual teachings to help improve the lives of poor people. Ron Packard, a Republican congressman from California, writes, "Unlike a government handout, where the value is gone as soon as the money is spent, local and faith-based charities provide hope by restoring trust, building relationships and touching souls."

Not everyone sees giving private charities all the responsibility for helping the poor as the best solution. Supporters of government programs express concern that private charities alone cannot provide enough aid to the poor. For example, many argue that Americans will not donate enough money for these organizations to be effective. Americans are not stingy; they donated approximately $159 billion to nonprofit groups in 1997. However, commentators point out, these nonprofit groups include not only charities focused on helping the poor but museums, universities, and cultural institutions as well. Furthermore, according to columnist Richard Cohen, these charities will not find enough Americans willing to serve as staff members or volunteers, especially in impoverished, crime-ridden neighborhoods. "If charity is going to only stay close to home, then the inner city, the reservation, the Appalachian hamlet are going to become even harsher places," he argues.

Regardless of the source of help, it is widely agreed that the poor do need assistance in order to become economically self-sufficient. In the following chapter, the authors debate what methods are best able to achieve this end.

"Critics will say that the United States does not have the money for . . . a Marshall Plan for its poor. To them I say we cannot afford not to enact these measures."

GOVERNMENT POLICIES ARE NEEDED TO HELP THE POOR

Ruth Sidel

In the following viewpoint, Ruth Sidel maintains that the best solution for poverty is a universal family policy funded by the government. This policy, Sidel explains, would provide cash payments for families with children, health care, child care, and other services that would improve the lives of American families, especially the poorer ones. Although Sidel admits that such a policy could be expensive, she contends that the current costs of poverty—including homeless shelters, drug addiction, and crime—are far costlier in the long run. Sidel is a nationwide speaker on women's issues and a professor of sociology at Hunter College in New York City. She is the author of the book *Keeping Women and Children Last: America's War on the Poor*, from which the following viewpoint is excerpted.

As you read, consider the following questions:

1. In Sidel's view, what does "welfare reform" actually mean?
2. How many children under the age of thirteen lack adult supervision before or after school, according to the author?
3. According to statistics cited by Sidel, how many households do not receive housing aid they are eligible for?

The question for the United States today is what social and economic policies will most effectively help families in our extremely affluent society to live decent lives without the specter of poverty hovering over them. Should a family policy stress universal benefits? Should policies be targeted for specific at-risk groups or should we move toward a combination of the two approaches? Many other countries use a complex combination of tax policy, employment policy, universal social policy, and specific programs targeted to the most vulnerable. Sweden, for example, has focused on employment policies and universal benefits which combine to produce extremely low rates of poverty. The Netherlands has low rates of poverty for women because it has developed a generous social policy that provides a relatively high income floor for all citizens. Poverty rates are low for Dutch women because poverty rates are low for all Dutch citizens.

WOMEN'S AMBIGUOUS ROLES

In thinking through an appropriate U.S. family policy for the twenty-first century, we must recognize that most mothers today, particularly single mothers, are caught in a difficult and often painful role conflict that is exacerbated by the unwillingness of American society to recognize and respond to the real needs of families. As Lydia Morris, author of *Dangerous Classes: The Underclass and Social Citizenship,* has pointed out,

> Recent developments in the conceptualization of citizenship have increasingly placed at least as much emphasis on obligations as on rights, the prime obligation being work as a means to independence. This places women in an ambiguous position: either they earn their "public" citizenship rights by their own paid employment, or they perform their "private" family obligations and remain dependent. This conflict can only be resolved by a redistribution of the "private" obligations of unpaid labour, or by some acknowledgement of the "public" service such labour performs, or by increasing state involvement in the "private" obligation to care for children.

This is exactly where the United States stands today. Women are still expected to care for the home and particularly for the children but they are increasingly expected to participate in the paid labor market. In most two-parent families women's income has helped keep the family afloat as men's wages have declined over the past two decades. But while virtually all of the Western European countries have developed a panoply of social supports for families, American society has not seen fit to redistribute the private obligations of women on a significant scale either to men or to the public sector. What "welfare reform" really means is that women are being forced to take on both roles full-time without either adequate salaries or adequate help in providing for their children. Many mothers must provide care and love and food and clothing and values and discipline while holding down a full-time job and earning wages either below or close to the poverty line. They are increasingly expected to do all this both without the help of a man, since many of the men are nowhere to be found, and without the help of the society.

WOMEN NEED ASSISTANCE

As Lester Thurow, professor of economics at the Massachusetts Institute of Technology, has written,

> Whether it is fathering a family without being willing to be a father, whether it is divorce and being unwilling to pay alimony or child support, or whether it is being an immigrant from the third world and after a time failing to send payments to the family back home, men all around the world are opting out.

In addition, policies adopted by state and federal levels of government in the United States mean that the society is opting out as well. What we are asking of women is virtually impossible. It would be exceedingly difficult under the best of circumstances—with family supports, a living wage, and adequate benefits. Yet, poor women often have none of these.

In *Women and Children Last,* I called for a universal family policy—one that would simultaneously reach all Americans and target the most vulnerable among us with special programs. It may seem quixotic at best and foolhardy at worst to propose a universal family policy at a time when conservatism is in the ascendancy, when government programs are viewed with widespread pessimism and even cynicism, and when the United States has incurred a massive deficit. Nonetheless, we need nothing short of this today.

A POLICY FOR ALL FAMILIES

A universal family policy should include, I believe, children's allowances. As in many European countries, every family, regardless of income, should receive a flat amount per child under the age of eighteen. This transfer would indicate that we all have a stake in the well-being of every child; it would help families when funds are particularly low, but would not be a large enough amount to provide an incentive for having additional children. We might want to consider the amount taxable for affluent families, but the principle of universalism is important nevertheless.

America's families must have comprehensive, affordable health care whether through a system of national health insurance or a national health service. All of our families need prenatal care, well-baby care, immunizations, access to contraception and abortion services, and health care for all family members including the elderly. Despite the fiasco of proposals for "health care reform" during the first two years of the Clinton Administration, a universal health care system must be a priority for America's families.

A Look at France's Welfare System

Among industrialized countries, the United States is alone in having no universal preschool, child-support, or parental leave programs. . . .

The French system of child welfare stands in sharp contrast to the American system. In France, children are supported by three interrelated government programs—child care, income support, and medical care. The child care program includes establishments for infant care, high-quality nursery schools (*écoles maternelles*), and paid leave for parents of newborns. The income support program includes child-support enforcement (so that the absent parent continues to contribute financially to his or her child's welfare), children allowances, and welfare payments for low-income single mothers. Finally, medical care is provided through a universal system of national health care financed by social security, a preventive care system for children, and a group of public health nurses who specialize in child welfare.

William Julius Wilson, *When Work Disappears: The World of the New Urban Poor*, 1996.

We should consider instituting paid, parental leave for all parents at the time of the birth or adoption of a baby. If such leave is unpaid, as it is now for millions of workers, only the affluent or members of two-parent families can afford to take it. Sweden currently offers a twelve-month leave of which one month must be taken by the father. We, too, should consider ways of encouraging fathers to participate more fully in child rearing from the time of the birth of the baby and even, when possible, during pregnancy. Everyone will gain—fathers, mothers who desperately need to share child rearing responsibilities, and the children; sharing parenting more fully may well give the family unit a greater sense of cohesion.

First-rate, accessible, affordable child care must also be a priority. With the vast majority of women, including mothers of preschoolers, currently participating in the paid labor force, public, private, and nonprofit institutions must work together to establish a variety of child-care options, including after-school care, with priority going to working parents, to parents who are students, to single parents, and to parents with special needs. The urgency of after-school care is clear; an estimated 2 million children under the age of thirteen have no adult supervision either before or after school. Moreover, if these are truly creative environments in which children can explore, socialize with one another and with their caregivers, and be nourished physically, emotionally, and intellectually, the entire society will benefit in the long run.

Housing and Education Reforms

With at least 1 million Americans, including a growing number of children and working adults, homeless at some time each year, the United States must rethink its housing policy. As Peter Dreier, Distinguished Professor of Politics at Occidental College, and John Atlas, attorney and president of the National Housing Institute, note, "Among Western democracies, the U.S. relies most heavily on private market forces to house its population." They point out that while the United States provides more than $100 billion a year to housing subsidies, by far the largest amount, $64 billion, goes to mortgage interest and property tax reduction for home owners while $13 billion goes to tax breaks for wealthy investors in rental housing and mortgage revenue bonds. They further point out that only 4.1 million low-income households receive aid while twice as many, 9.7 million households, are eligible but do not receive any help. Dreier and Atlas call for a policy that would spend the same money we are spending now but would target that money for those most in need.

And, of course, our grossly unequal system of education must be reformed. If we really believe in fairness, in equality of opportunity, we must consider how to restructure a system that provides every opportunity imaginable for the privileged while other young people are left to grow up virtually ignored and illiterate, discarded as disposable in a society dominated by the need for technology and sophisticated expertise. Until these children are educated for life in the twenty-first century, they will live at the margins of society and we will all, in the long run, be the losers. . . .

Preventing Future Ills

Critics will say that the United States does not have the money for a comprehensive family policy, for decent housing and education and health care for all, for a Marshall Plan [the United States' effort to rehabilitate Europe after World War II] for its poor. To them I say we cannot afford not to enact these measures. Moreover, we are spending the money now in other ways. We are spending it on jails and prisons; we are spending it on treating tuberculosis and lead poisoning. We are spending it on low-birth-weight babies and learning disabilities. We are spending it on the effects of addiction and violence, on a largely bankrupt welfare system, on an inadequate foster care system, and on shelters for the homeless. We are spending it on wasted human potential.

Finally, there is strong evidence that these policies save money in the long run. This is perhaps clearest in issues involving health status: adequate, early, comprehensive prenatal care is surely cheaper—and of course more humane—than dealing with the often severe complications of low-birth-weight babies; immunizations are clearly more cost-efficient than treating the consequences of preventable childhood diseases; and routing out lead-based paint in housing and schools is less costly both in dollars and in preserving human potential than permitting children to suffer from lead poisoning. In virtually all other areas prevention is cheaper than dealing with the consequences of severe, preventable individual, family, and societal problems. Keeping families together is far cheaper than foster care and vastly less expensive than any form of institutionalization. First-rate education costs the society less than maintaining families who cannot adequately support themselves. An entire panoply of human services is less costly—in every sense—than drug and alcohol programs and markedly less costly than incarceration. It is thus in the society's best interest—in human terms as well as financial terms— to help individuals and families function effectively.

"Private charity is ennobling of
everyone involved, both those who
give and those who receive.
Government welfare is ennobling of
no one."

PRIVATE CHARITIES CAN BEST HELP
THE POOR

Michael Tanner

Michael Tanner is the director of health and welfare studies at
the Cato Institute, a libertarian public policy research foundation
in Washington, D.C. In the following viewpoint, Tanner asserts
that private charities, rather than government welfare programs,
are best suited to help the poor. He contends that private charities are a superior solution because they can offer individualized
help and promote religious values. In contrast, Tanner argues,
government programs are bogged down in faceless bureaucracy.
Charity should be a voluntary and ennobling act, rather than an
obligation forced upon a nation's citizens, he maintains. Tanner
is the author of the book *The End of Welfare: Fighting Poverty in the Civil
Society*, from which this viewpoint is excerpted.

As you read, consider the following questions:

1. What percentage of American adults make charitable
   contributions each year, according to Tanner?
2. According to the author, what percentage of families living
   below the poverty level do not receive government
   assistance?
3. In Tanner's view, why do people give in a civil society?

Reprinted, by permission, from Michael Tanner, *The End of Welfare: Fighting Poverty in the Civil
Society* (Washington, DC: Cato Institute), ©1996, the Cato Institute.

P rivate efforts have been much more successful than the federal government's failed attempt at charity. America is the most generous nation on earth. Americans already contribute more than $125 billion annually to charity. In fact, more than 85 percent of all adult Americans make some charitable contribution each year. In addition, about half of all American adults perform volunteer work; more than 20 billion hours were worked in 1991. The dollar value of that volunteer work was more than $176 billion. Volunteer work and cash donations combined bring American charitable contributions to more than $300 billion per year, not including the countless dollars and time given informally to family members, neighbors, and others outside the formal charity system.

MEETING INDIVIDUAL NEEDS

Private charities have been more successful than government welfare for several reasons. First, private charities are able to individualize their approach to the circumstances of poor people in ways that governments can never do. Government regulations must be designed to treat all similarly situated recipients alike. Glenn C. Loury of Boston University explains the difference between welfare and private charities on that point. "Because citizens have due process rights which cannot be fully abrogated . . . public judgments must be made in a manner that can be defended after the fact, sometimes even in court." The result is that most government programs rely on the simple provision of cash or other goods and services without any attempt to differentiate between the needs of recipients.

Take, for example, the case of a poor person who has a job offer. But she can't get to the job because her car battery is dead. A government welfare program can do nothing but tell her to wait two weeks until her welfare check arrives. Of course, by that time the job will be gone. A private charity can simply go out and buy a car battery (or even jump-start the dead battery).

The sheer size of government programs works against individualization. As one welfare case worker lamented, "With 125 cases it's hard to remember that they're all human beings. Sometimes they're just a number." Bureaucracy is a major factor in government welfare programs. For example, a report on welfare in Illinois found procedures requiring "nine forms to process an address change, at least six forms to add or delete a member of a household, and a minimum of six forms to report a change in earnings or employment." All that for just one program.

In her excellent book *Tyranny of Kindness*, Theresa Funiciello, a former welfare mother, describes the dehumanizing world of the government welfare system—a system in which regulations and bureaucracy rule all else. It is a system in which illiterate homeless people with mental illnesses are handed 17-page forms to fill out, women nine months pregnant are told to verify their pregnancies, a woman who was raped is told she is ineligible for benefits because she can't list the baby's father on the required form. It is a world totally unable to adjust to the slightest deviation from the bureaucratic norm.

In addition to being better able to target individual needs, private charities are much better able to target assistance to those who really need help. Because eligibility requirements for government welfare programs are arbitrary and cannot be changed to fit individual circumstances, many people in genuine need do not receive assistance, while benefits often go to people who do not really need them. More than 40 percent of all families living below the poverty level receive no government assistance. Yet more than half of the families receiving means-tested benefits are not poor. Thus, a student may receive food stamps, while a homeless man with no mailing address goes without. Private charities are not bound by such bureaucratic restrictions.

Private charity also has a better record of actually delivering aid to recipients. Surprisingly little of the money being spent on federal and state social welfare programs actually reaches recipients. In 1965, 70 cents of every dollar spent by the government to fight poverty went directly to poor people. Today, 70 cents of every dollar goes, not to poor people, but to government bureaucrats and others who serve the poor. Few private charities have the bureaucratic overhead and inefficiency of government programs.

PRIVATE CHARITIES PROMOTE VALUES

Second, in general, private charity is much more likely to be targeted to short-term emergency assistance than to long-term dependence. Thus, private charity provides a safety net, not a way of life.

Moreover, private charities may demand that the poor change their behavior in exchange for assistance. For example, a private charity may reduce or withhold benefits if a recipient does not stop using alcohol or drugs, look for a job, or avoid pregnancy. Private charities are much more likely than government programs to offer counseling and one-on-one follow-up rather than simply provide a check.

By the same token, because of the separation of church and

state, government welfare programs are not able to support programs that promote religious values as a way out of poverty. Yet church and other religious charities have a history of success in dealing with the problems that often lead to poverty.

Chuck Asay and Creators Syndicate, reprinted by permission.

Finally, and perhaps most important, private charity requires a different attitude on the part of both recipients and donors. For recipients, private charity is not an entitlement but a gift carrying reciprocal obligations. As Father Robert Sirico of the Acton Institute describes it, "An impersonal check given without any expectations for responsible behavior leads to a damaged sense of self-worth. The beauty of local [private charitable] efforts to help the needy is that . . . they make the individual receiving the aid realize that he must work to live up to the expectations of those helping him out."

Private charity demands that donors become directly involved. Former Yale University political science professor James Payne notes how little citizen involvement there is in government charity:

We know now that in most cases of government policy making, decisions are not made according to the democratic ideal of control by ordinary citizens. Policy is made by elites, through special interest politics, bureaucratic pressures, and legislative manipulations. Insiders decide what happens, shaping the outcome according to their own preferences and their political pull. The citizens are simply bystanders.

Private charity, in contrast, is based on "having individuals vote with their own time, money, and energy."

There is no compassion in spending someone else's money— even for a good cause. True compassion means giving of yourself. As historian and social commentator Gertrude Himmelfarb puts it, "Compassion is a moral sentiment, not a political principle." Welfare allows individuals to escape their obligation to be truly charitable. As Robert Thompson of the University of Pennsylvania said a century ago, government charity is a "rough contrivance to lift from the social conscience a burden that should not be either lifted or lightened in that way."

That is the essence of the civil society. When George Washington contrasted government to civil society in his farewell address, warning that "government is not reason, it is not eloquence—it is force," he was making an important distinction. Government relies on force and coercion to achieve its objectives, including charity. In contrast, the civil society relies on persuasion—reason and eloquence—to motivate voluntary giving. In the civil society people give because they are committed to helping, because they believe in what they are doing.

GOVERNMENT RELIEF IS IMPERSONAL

Thus private charity is ennobling of everyone involved, both those who give and those who receive. Government welfare is ennobling of no one. Alexis de Tocqueville recognized that 150 years ago. Calling for the abolition of public relief, Tocqueville lauded private charity for establishing a "moral tie" between giver and receiver. In contrast, impersonal government relief destroys any sense of morality. The donor (read taxpayer) resents his involuntary contribution, while the recipient feels no gratitude for what he receives and inevitably believes that what he receives is insufficient.

Perhaps the entire question of government welfare versus private charity was best summed up by Pope John Paul II in his encyclical *Centesimus Annus*.

> By intervening directly and depriving society of its responsibility, the welfare state leads to a loss of human energies and an inordinate increase in public agencies, which are dominated more by bureaucratic ways of thinking than by concern for serving their clients, and which are accompanied by an enormous increase in spending. In fact, it would appear that needs are best understood and satisfied by people who are closest to them and who act as

neighbors to those in need. It should be added that certain kinds of demands often call for a response which is not material but which is capable of perceiving the deeper human need.

Better yet, consider this simple thought experiment: If you had $10,000 available that you wanted to use to help the poor, would you give it to the government to help fund welfare or would you donate it to the private charity of your choice?

| "The most important question is ... how society should allocate scarce housing resources in order to do the most good and cause the least suffering."

SAFER PUBLIC HOUSING WOULD HELP THE POOR

Dennis Saffran

Many poor people live in public housing projects subsidized by the federal government. Because these projects are often the site of drug dealing, gang violence, and other crimes, new policies have been enacted that make it easier to screen out and evict residents who engage in criminal activities. In the following viewpoint, Dennis Saffran argues that these policies are necessary in order to allow impoverished, law-abiding families to reside in public housing without the fear of living amid criminals. Saffran is the New York director of the Center for the Community Interest and the former general counsel of the New York State Division of Housing and Community Renewal.

As you read, consider the following questions:

1. What does the "innocent grandmother" argument ignore, according to Saffran?
2. Why is it ineffective to evict just the criminal rather than the entire household where the criminal resides, according to the author?
3. In Saffran's view, what fundamental flaw do the arguments against toughened eviction policies share?

Reprinted from Dennis Saffran, "Public Housing Safety Versus Tenants' Rights," *Responsive Community*, Fall 1996, by permission.

On the evening of Sunday, August 27, 1995, 4-year-old Shamone Johnson was caught in the crossfire between two rival drug gangs and killed while roller-skating outside her godmother's home in a Brooklyn housing project. Recent actions by Congress and President Bill Clinton, and by a federal judge in New York, will finally make it easier for public housing authorities to protect poor children like Shamone from this kind of vicious drug-related violence. Yet these actions are staunchly opposed by some groups that claim to be champions of the poor.

TOUGHER SCREENING RULES

In March 1996, the president signed the Housing Opportunity Program Extension ("HOPE") Act of 1996, which strengthens the ability of federally subsidized housing projects to screen out and evict drug dealers and other criminals who prey on their law-abiding neighbors. And he announced a "One Strike And You're Out" policy, which encourages housing authorities to take full advantage of these new powers. Under the policy, an authority's receipt of federal funds will be based, in part, on its use of a lease that clearly provides that any drug-related or other serious criminal activity by a member of a household is grounds for eviction. The policy also encourages housing authorities to more effectively screen applicants for admission by using access to federal and state criminal conviction records provided by the HOPE Act.

The "One Strike" policy was drafted by [former] Housing and Urban Development Secretary Henry Cisneros, one of the more liberal members of the Clinton administration. He noted that "the number one group of people" demanding such toughened public housing eviction and screening rules "are the residents themselves," who have been forced to "put children to sleep in bathtubs" (to protect them from stray bullets) and otherwise abandon their rights and their dignity. Yet the policy was branded as unconstitutional by the American Civil Liberties Union.

While the One Strike policy has not been officially challenged, a court case in New York earlier in 1996 involved similar issues. In April 1996, the New York City Housing Authority (the nation's largest provider of low-income housing) and tenant leaders represented by the American Alliance for Rights and Responsibilities prevailed in their attempt to modify a 25-year-old federal court decree that had made it particularly difficult to evict drug dealers from public housing in New York. The 1971 consent decree in the *Escalera* case required the Housing Authority to go through a lengthy two-step eviction proceeding lasting up to two years. This made it impossible for the Authority to take advantage of New York State's "Bawdy House Law," which allows for expedited eviction proceedings (without abandoning due process protections) in drug cases. Efforts by the administrations of both former Mayor David Dinkins and current Mayor Rudolph Giuliani to modify the 1971 decree were vigorously opposed by the Legal Services Corporation and the Legal Aid Society, who argued that no change was called for because "the incidence of drug-related crime is not significantly different today than in the 1970s." This argument was squarely rejected both by the court and by the elected tenant representatives, which intervened in the case in support of modifying the decree.

THE ALLOCATION DILEMMA

Opponents of these reforms have largely abandoned the argument that the drug dealers themselves have a right to remain in public housing. Rather, they raise the specter of innocent family members who may face eviction as the result of the illegal activity of a member of their household. This "innocent grandmother" argument seems compelling, but it ignores a simple and more compelling reality: *public housing is a scarce resource available only to a fraction of the poor people who desperately need it.* This means that criteria other than need alone must be used to determine who gets this housing. There are three poor families on the waiting list for every unit of public housing, and the vast majority are fully law-abiding and therefore would not endanger the safety of other tenants. Thus, as John Atlas and Peter Dreier have noted in *The American Prospect*, the screening and eviction of problem families "does not exclude more tenants; it simply gives priority to certain tenants on criteria other than first come, first serve."

In this situation, the most important question is not whether a grandmother or other family member of a drug dealer is completely innocent or tacitly acquiescent, but rather how society should allocate scarce housing resources in order to do the most good and cause the least suffering. Looked at in this way, the choice between a poor family that, however innocently, has let its apartment be used as a base of operations for terrorizing its neighbors, and an equally poor family on the waiting list that would not pose such a threat, is a painful one but a clear one. As President Clinton stated in announcing the One Strike policy: "The people who are living [in public housing] deserve to be protected, and the good people who want to live [there] deserve to have a chance," and it is therefore "morally wrong" to allow households harboring criminals "to use up homes that could make a big difference in the lives of decent families." The same point was made in *Edison v. Pierce* by a federal appellate court in upholding the screening of undesirable tenants from participation in the Section 8 housing voucher program:

> At the heart of this case is the fact that there are not enough . . . housing units to accommodate all who are eligible. . . . At issue are the rights not only of those . . . who were denied . . . benefits but also of those who received those benefits in the[ir] stead.

But, opponents respond, why not require only the criminal to move rather than evicting the entire household? In fact, both the One Strike policy and the New York Bawdy House Law that was at issue in *Escalera* do allow for such individualized discretion in the case of tenants who were genuinely unable to prevent the use of their apartments for criminal activity. In such situations, the family may be allowed to remain on the condition that it agree to a permanent order of exclusion barring the offender from the premises. The hard truth, however, is that this approach needs to be used sparingly because it usually does not work—and it is actually least likely to work in those cases in which the plight of the tenant-of-record is the most sympathetic. The drug dealers, gang members, and other criminals subject to these orders of exclusion are not the kind of people who tend to have a lot of respect for such documents, especially since the sanction for violation is directed against their families rather than against them personally. And it is precisely those thugs who bullied, intimidated, and if necessary beat their families into complicity in their illegal activity—that is, those whose families are most truly innocent—who are the *least* likely to remain away from profitable turf out of either respect for the law or tender concern that grandma might lose her apartment.

CRIME AND THE EVICTION PROCESS

The One Strike policy and the Bawdy House Law provide tenants with the right to a hearing on the charges of illegal activity prior to eviction, but do not require a criminal conviction on these charges. Opponents point to this as a grievous violation of rights—an argument that has a surface appeal but is ultimately specious. As stated by Assistant Attorney General Walter Dellinger, a former law professor with a reputation as a staunch civil libertarian and liberal:

> Eviction is a civil, not a criminal matter. Tenants in both public and private housing are subject to eviction for violations of appropriate lease terms, whether it is keeping an unlawful pet or violating any of the other reasonable terms of a lease. Lease

terms prohibiting [criminal] activities like this are no different. The fact that no conviction is required does not leave public housing authorities free to evict tenants on the basis of speculation or suspicion [since] tenants have . . . the right to a hearing.

The criminal standard of "proof beyond a reasonable doubt" has never been required in eviction proceedings, or in any other civil proceedings based on conduct that could also be criminally actionable. And, as a practical matter, allowing a drug-dealing or gun-toting tenant to remain on the premises for months or years while awaiting the outcome of a criminal proceeding would largely undermine the goal of removing dangerous persons from public housing, while increasing the very real risk of witness intimidation.

A PATRONIZING ATTITUDE

Perhaps more importantly, the two main arguments against toughened eviction policies—that public housing tenants should not be held responsible for the illegal activities of members of their households, and should not be subject to eviction for these activities based on the same civil standard of proof applicable to evictions from private housing—also share a flaw more fundamental than those discussed above. That flaw is the patronizing and destructive refusal to apply to low-income communities the same standards that maintain social order and well-being in middle-income neighborhoods—and that for many years did so in poor areas as well. It is not uncommon for tenants to be evicted from private housing based on the misconduct of their children in violation of the lease, regardless of whether the misconduct has been criminally proven or even constitutes a crime. In the middle-income apartment building in which I grew up in Queens, New York, for example, there was a three-strikes-and-you're-out policy for petty mischief like defacing property or even ball playing in the halls. (A one-strike policy for serious criminal activity was implicit.) This policy did have a harsh impact on the often blameless parents of trouble-making children, but it allowed the rest of us to grow up in decent and safe surroundings.

Similar and even stricter rules of conduct, punishable by eviction, were enforced in public housing in that era (the late fifties and early sixties) and, not coincidentally, the projects then still provided about as good an environment in which to raise children as did any middle-income development. Indeed, public housing worked in this country for 30 years—filling a void left by the private market and providing tens of thousands with a safe, clean, and stable oasis in which to gain a foothold out of poverty. This is an inconvenient bit of history for both the free market absolutists who need to face the fact that a government program worked, and the doctrinaire liberals who need to confront why it *stopped* working. It stopped working when well-intentioned civil libertarians, responding to genuine excesses in which public housing rules had been applied in arbitrary and sometimes racially insensitive ways, pushed the pendulum to the other extreme. In a series of court decisions and decrees, followed by legislative and administrative changes that interpreted these decisions as expansively as possible, the civil rights and civil liberties bar won victories that seriously restricted the ability of housing authorities to achieve certain previously accepted goals: to screen out and evict criminals and other undesirable or disruptive tenants; to give preference to intact and working families; or even to maintain a healthy balance between the working and welfare poor. The unintended result was a breakdown of the social order that had allowed public housing to succeed in the first place.

The One Strike policy and the *Escalera* decision are two big steps towards moving the pendulum back to the center and restoring public housing to the success story that it once was. These developments offer the hope that some day little children growing up in the projects may once again enjoy the same right that my own 4-year-old daughter and other middle-class children now have to play outside their homes without fear of random, violent death. Why should advocates for civil liberties and the poor oppose that?

| "Housing subsidies undermine the efforts of those poor families who work and sacrifice to advance their lot in life."

SUBSIDIZED PUBLIC HOUSING SHOULD BE ELIMINATED

Howard Husock

In the following viewpoint, Howard Husock contends that subsidized public housing has failed and should be replaced by the private housing market. Husock argues that public housing has expensive maintenance costs and establishes unrealistic building codes and zoning laws that lead to housing shortages. In addition, he asserts, subsidized public housing does not allow poor families to create better neighborhoods through their own hard work. A housing policy that offers different levels of housing and does not have unnecessary building codes would be the best solution for the housing shortage, according to Husock. Husock is the director of the Case Study Program at Harvard University's John F. Kennedy School of Government in Cambridge, Massachusetts.

As you read, consider the following questions:

1. What are the two approaches to public housing in the current era, according to Husock?
2. According to a study by the New School for Social Research, as cited by the author, what percentage of nonprofit housing developments have maintenance problems?
3. Why is subsidized housing more expensive than it first appears, according to the author?

Reprinted, by permission, from Howard Husock, "We Don't Need Subsidized Housing." This article first appeared in the Winter 1997 issue of *City Journal*.

Devoting government resources to subsidized housing for the poor—whether in the form of public housing or even housing vouchers—is not just unnecessary but also counterproductive. It not only derails what the private market can do on its own, but more significantly, it has profoundly destructive unintended consequences. For housing subsidies undermine the efforts of those poor families who work and sacrifice to advance their lot in life—and who have the right and the need to distinguish themselves, both physically and psychologically, from those who do not share their solid virtues.

A History of Failed Approaches

Rather than confront these harsh truths, we have over the past century gone through at least five major varieties of subsidized housing, always looking for the philosophers' stone that will turn a bad idea into one that will work. We began with philanthropic housing built by "limited dividend" corporations, whose investors were to accept a below-market return in order to serve the poor. The disappointing results of such efforts—the projects served few people and tended to decline quickly—led housing advocates to call for public, not just private, spending for housing. Government first responded to their pleas with housing projects owned and operated by public authorities. These speedily declined. "Housers" then sought other solutions, such as using cheap, federally underwritten mortgages and rents paid by Washington to subsidize private landlords.

The expense of this last approach, which had its heyday in the sixties, and the resultant wave of decline and foreclosure led to the twin approaches of our current era. In the first of these, tenants use portable, government-provided vouchers to pay any private landlord who will accept them. In the second, federal tax credits encourage deep-pocketed corporate investors looking for tax shelters to finance new or renovated rental housing owned and managed by nonprofit community groups. Both approaches have had serious problems, but this hasn't deterred housing advocates from asserting that the way to fix the housing market is through even more such subsidies than the $12 billion that the Department of Housing and Urban Development (HUD) already provides (out of its $25 billion annual budget) and the billions more in subsidies that state and local governments expend.

This mountain of government housing subsidies rests on three remarkably tenacious myths.

Myth No. 1: *The market will not provide.* The core belief of housing advocates is that the private market cannot and will not provide adequate housing within the means of the poor. The photos of immigrants squeezed into postage-stamp-sized rooms in a recent *New York Times* series on housing for the poor strain to make this point. But trousers have been making such assertions for more than 60 years, and reality keeps contradicting them. In 1935, for example, Catherine Bauer—perhaps America's most influential public housing crusader—claimed that the private housing market could not serve fully two-thirds of Americans and they would need public housing. The post–World War II era's explosion of home ownership quickly gave the lie to such claims, certainly with respect to those in the lower middle class and up. . . .

THE PITFALLS OF STRINGENT STANDARDS

Perversely, housing reformers invariably make matters worse by banning the conditions that shock them. Insisting unrealistically on standards beyond the financial means of the poor, they help create housing shortages, which they then seek to remedy through public subsidies. Even Jacob Riis observed in 1907 that new tenement standards threatened "to make it impossible for anyone not able to pay $75 a month to live on Manhattan Island."

Though Riis's colleague Lawrence Veiller, head of the influential New York–based National Housing Association from 1900 to 1920, cautioned that "housing legislation must distinguish between what is desirable and what is essential," most housing programs since the New Deal have rejected this sensible advice. The high standards that have resulted—whether for the number of closets, the square feet of kitchen counter space, or handicapped access—have caused private owners and builders to bypass the low-income market. So stringent are the standards that, under current building codes and zoning laws, much of the distinctive lower-cost housing that shaped the architectural identity of America's cities—such as Brooklyn's attached brownstones with basement apartments—could not be built today.

True, even with relaxed building and housing codes, we still might not be able to build brand-new housing within the reach of those earning the minimum wage or those living on public assistance. Yet this is not an irresistible argument for government subsidies. Used housing, like used cars, gets passed along to those of more and more modest means. When new homes are built for the lower middle class, the rental housing in which they've been living (itself probably inherited from the middle class) historically has been passed along to those who are poorer.

In a subtle way, the very existence of subsidized housing is likely to contribute to the over-regulation that leads to constraints in housing supply—and to calls for further subsidies. When builders have plenty of work putting up high-cost subsidized apartments, they don't agitate for a less regulated market. Why should they seek an opportunity to build lower-margin low-cost housing? The rejoinder, then, to the myth that the market will not provide is that a greater supply of housing could be—and has been—created in a less regulated market.

Reprinted by permission of Jerry Barnett.

Myth No. 2: *By taking profit-driven landlords out of the equation, state-supported housing can offer the poor higher-quality housing for the same rent.* Four generations of attempts to provide subsidized housing built to higher standards than the poor court effort on their own in the private market have proved that this idea just doesn't work. Each generation has seen the same depressing pattern: initial success followed by serious decline and ultimately by demands for additional public funds to cover ever-rising costs. . . .

The new public housing motel that advocates favor retains the core—and fatal—dogma that the profit motive has no place in providing housing for the poor. In this motel, nonprofit community groups run smaller, mixed-income apartment buildings, financed by monies raised through the Low-Income Housing

Tax Credit, a program set up in 1986 to encourage corporations to support low-income housing. In New York City some 200 nonprofit groups manage 48,000 housing units. Though at this point such housing is widely viewed as successful, the New School for Social Research has found, in an examination of 34 developments in six cities, that "beyond an initial snapshot of well-being, loom major problems which, if unaddressed, will threaten the stock of affordable housing in this study." Predictably enough, more than 60 percent of the projects already had trouble maintaining their paint and plaster, elevators, hall lighting and roofs.

Why does non-market housing founder? First, providing the poor with better housing than they can afford also saddles them with higher maintenance costs than they can afford. A newly announced state-financed "affordable housing" complex in Cambridge, Massachusetts, will cost $1.3 million—for eight units. That's $162,500 per apartment. Recent subsidized projects in the Bronx and central Harlem cost $150,000 and $113,000 per unit, respectively. These apartments may be built to higher standards, but their fancier kitchens, more numerous bathrooms, and larger space mean more maintenance. Not surprisingly, limited rents can't keep up with the need for service. . . .

COMPARING HOUSING COSTS

Second, it is by no means true that cutting out the profit-making landlord reduces maintenance costs. On the contrary, public authorities and nonprofit management firms are bureaucracies with their own overhead expenses, and unlike private owners, they have no incentive to control costs. Nor have their employees any incentive to provide good service; and tenants, who are not full-fledged paying customers, have little leverage. Indeed, public housing authorities have demonstrated an ability rivaling any slumlord to disinvest in their properties.

Rather than being a source of ill-gotten gains, private ownership is a source of cost control. The expensive but ineffective maintenance regime of subsidized housing—with its formal bids and union contracts—replaces housing maintenance performed through a far less costly informal economy. Poor homeowners and so-called "tenement landlords" (owners of small, multi-family buildings, many owner-occupied) contribute their own "sweat equity" or hire neighborhood tradesmen, not all of whom are licensed, let alone unionized. As one study of a low-income neighborhood in Montreal observed, "Owners can maintain their buildings and keep their rents low through the cooperation of their tenants on maintenance and through their own hard work." None of these factors comes into play in the bureaucratic environment of public or nonprofit ownership.

Far from being more cost-effective than private housing, subsidized housing is even more expensive than it first appears. Its cost includes the vast amount of property-tax revenue forgone when rental housing is held by public authorities or non-tax-paying nonprofit groups. By choosing to invest in housing, cities choose not to invest in other services, or not to leave money in the private economy to finance growth that would provide opportunity for poor and non-poor alike. . . .

The rejoinder, then, to the myth of the public or nonprofit alternative is that gleaming new projects are bound to decay—and to have significant long-term public costs. But for housing advocates, this is really just a political problem: that of making clear to the body politic that perpetually escalating subsidies to guarantee a safe and sanitary environment for the poor are the cost of living in a moral body politic. Here we arrive at the nub of their mistaken ideology.

PUBLIC HOUSING DOES NOT IMPROVE BEHAVIOR

Myth No. 3: *The moral qualities of the poor are a product of their housing "environment."* The essence of the housing advocates' worldview, as the New York Association for Improving the Condition of the Poor put it in 1854, is that "physical evils produce moral evils." Improved physical surroundings will lead people to become upright, ambitious, and successful. Perhaps the quintessential myth of environmental determinism is that kids who might otherwise have no place to do their homework have their own room in government-assisted housing—and therefore succeed where they would have failed.

There is much that is appealing in this view, which has a powerful hold on the liberal psyche. But the track record of public housing—which by almost any physical measure is superior to the housing in which most of its residents have previously lived—has hardly borne out the notion that better housing uplifts the poor. The response of housing reformers to drug- and gunfire-riddled projects has been not to re-examine the premise but to tinker with the model. Having long dwelled on design, they now devote equal attention to the social "environment." Thus [former Housing] Secretary Henry Cisneros has dreamed of new, low-rise, mixed-income subsidized housing that will correct the mistake of concentrating the poor in apartment towers now said to have encouraged crime. So, too, the nonprofit, "community-based" management of renovated apartment buildings is touted as a nurturing environment, in which the poorest are inspired by gainfully employed "role-model" neighbors to improve their habits and their lot.

Here is where housing advocates most radically misunderstand the nature of the unsubsidized housing market. They can't see its crucial role in weaving a healthy social fabric and inspiring individuals to advance. By pushing to provide the poor with better housing than they could otherwise afford, housers are blind to the fact that they are interfering with a delicate system that rewards effort and achievement by giving people the chance to live in better homes in better neighborhoods. In this unsubsidized system, you earn your way to a better neighborhood. In fact, you must help to create and to maintain better neighborhoods by your own effort. . . .

The Working Poor Deserve Better

Subsidies deny the self-sacrificing, working poor the chance to put physical and social distance between themselves and the non-working or anti-social poor. The New York Times cited the case of a hardworking woman who found herself in a bad neighborhood surrounded by gang violence as evidence of the need for increased housing subsidies, but it more likely demonstrates the opposite. By subsidizing troubled families, perhaps with criminal members, so that they can live in the same neighborhoods as those who hold modest but honest jobs, we expose the law-abiding to the disorder and violence of the undisciplined and the lawless, depriving them of the decent neighborhood—decent in values if shabby in appearance—that their efforts should earn them. If we fail to allow the hardworking to distinguish themselves, by virtue of where they live, from those who do not share these traits, we devalue them. Even if we could somehow subsidize only the good citizens, the deserving poor, we would still do them a grave disservice, fostering the belief that they have moved to better homes in better neighborhoods by dint of largesse, not accomplishment—an entirely different psychology. . . .

True, the new subsidized projects run by community groups, with the advice of such sophisticated organizations as the Local Initiatives Support Corporation and the Enterprise Foundation, do seek to screen tenants so as to keep bad actors out of mixed-income developments. But it defies imagination to think that such a process will be as effective as the screening that the market does.

Indeed, in its analysis of such housing in New York, the New School found that though 6 percent of tenants were in arrears on their rent, the eviction rate was still zero.

A REALISTIC HOUSING SOLUTION

By remaining focused on the myth that physical conditions are the single most important quality of housing, housers have misunderstood the dynamics of neighborhoods—not merely as places where people live but as communities of shared ideals. As a result, they have blindly based new policies on old mistakes. Consider, for instance, recent housing initiatives that aim to promote racial integration by placing low-income minority families in apartments in the suburbs. These policies are a recipe for racial resentment, which has in fact developed. Asking working-class whites to accept the welfare poor—who would inspire discomfort whether white or black—as neighbors is the worst way to address the race issue. The right way is to enforce housing non-discrimination laws and thus allow the diffusion of upwardly mobile minority-group members into neighborhoods where, if they at first appear to be outsiders, it is only by virtue of race, not class.

A realistic housing policy would strive for a non-subsidized world in which many different sorts of housing form a housing ladder. The lower rungs will be modest indeed—as modest as the single-room-occupancy hotels that sprang up in San Diego when that city allowed dwellings with less-than-full bathrooms and limited parking. By relaxing its code requirements, the city catalyzed construction of some 2,700 new SRO units for the working poor—day laborers, cabdrivers, fast-food employees. The SROs have formed a housing ladder all their own: lower-rent buildings may have no TV or phone, while lobby guards in the better buildings enforce more stringent guest policies. A sensible housing policy would purge housing and building codes of unnecessary barriers to construction. . . .

In this new order, we would understand that a large, variegated supply is the way to restrain housing costs. We would understand that modest housing is a stage that people pass through—and that, by trying to stamp it out, we threaten to short-circuit the process by which they improve themselves. It is superficially attractive to give the hardworking breadwinner a leg up, a housing subsidy, to help pay the bills and raise his or her children. But in practice, because subsidies are provided on the basis of need, not effort or accomplishment, such a policy threatens not to solve our social problems but to make them permanent.

| "I believe small businesses will create the majority of new jobs for former welfare recipients."

SMALL BUSINESSES CAN HELP REDUCE POVERTY

Tom DeLay

In the following viewpoint, Tom DeLay contends that small businesses drive the economy and need entry-level workers in order to grow and succeed. However, he maintains, the complicated tax system and unwieldy government regulations discourage job creation. He concludes that small business can create jobs for poor people making the transition from welfare to work if the government reduces these costly regulations. DeLay is a Republican member of the U.S. House of Representatives from Texas.

As you read, consider the following questions:

1. According to DeLay, what are the two reasons why the private sector should create jobs?
2. What are DeLay's criticisms of make-work jobs?
3. What type of government do Americans need, according to the author?

Reprinted from Tom DeLay, "Putting People to Work Privately," *The Washington Times*, March 16, 1997, by permission.

In a March 1997 radio address to the American people, Bill Clinton announced that he would make the federal bureaucracy hire people who are currently on welfare. In his announcement, he said "government can help move people from welfare to work by acting the way we want all employers to act."

We all support the goal of putting people to work. But I disagree with the president when he says government must lead the way by inflating the government payroll to create jobs for people on welfare. I say the government can best lead this effort by getting out of the way.

CUTTING THE COSTS OF JOB CREATION

Small business is the engine that drives the economy, and I believe small businesses will create the majority of new jobs for former welfare recipients, but only if we let them by reducing unnecessary burdens to job creation.

I used to own a small business. I know how hard small business owners work to make ends meet, how government often hurts the bottom line, and how these entrepreneurs would like to hire additional workers but can't because the cost of hiring is so high.

Putting people to work doesn't have to be a partisan issue. In fact, I thought the president agreed that the private sector is the best place for people who are getting off welfare to get a job. In a meeting we had with him in February 1997, he said just that while acknowledging that creating jobs is too expensive for many employers. In fact, he said, "We must cut the marginal costs of employers for more job creation."

When he said that, I almost fell out of my chair. The president was singing my song. Coming from the man who signed an increase in the minimum wage and who oversees a bureaucracy that mounts ever more regulatory costs on our private sector, this sounded too good to be true. But perhaps if the president finally understands the end result of his actions means fewer jobs for entry-level workers, we have a chance to do something really extraordinary: Pass a bipartisan bill that creates jobs, expands economic growth, and works for all Americans.

THE FOUR PRINCIPLES OF JOB CREATION

Putting people to work, especially people who are able-bodied, who want to work, and who are currently on welfare, shouldn't be that hard, especially if our economy continues to grow. In my view, four principles must define this debate:

(1) *The private sector, not the government, must create the jobs:* This should be self-explanatory. But for many who yearn for the Franklin Delano Roosevelt (FDR) approach to job-creation, it is a revelation. The private sector needs to create the jobs for two simple reasons: First, the federal government can't afford a massive job program in this era of fiscal responsibility. Second, for our economy to continue to grow, it needs the full participation of all able-bodied Americans. The private sector needs entry-level workers today who will grow into the managers and entrepreneurs of tomorrow.

GOVERNMENT REGULATIONS CAUSE UNEMPLOYMENT

An important and overlooked factor in the continued high level of unemployment is the rising load of regulation, mandates, and payroll taxes that government is imposing on business and other employers. The direct cost of meeting employment mandates imposed by the federal government has been rising twice as fast as wages and salaries.

The indirect costs of employment regulations—many of which are both substantial and hidden—all share a common characteristic: they make adding workers to the payroll more expensive.

Murray Weidenbaum, *Freeman*, November 1994.

---

(2) *The jobs must be real, not make-work:* Our economy can't afford make-work jobs, and people who want to move from welfare don't want to work in make-work jobs. The dignity of work comes from accomplishing a task well. Getting paid for doing nothing diminishes the integrity of the worker as it diminishes the profits of the business. Entry-level jobs often include some unexciting tasks, but those tasks have to be done for the business to survive. Make-work jobs that don't contribute to the bottom line shouldn't be expected in a true welfare-to-work plan.

(3) *Allow jobs to flourish everywhere:* If our principal goal is putting people to work, the government shouldn't narrowly target who creates the jobs or where the jobs are created. I say let jobs flourish everywhere. Creating an atmosphere of job creation is like plowing a field for planting. It doesn't make sense to create good conditions in one area, while allowing horrible conditions to exist in another.

(4) *Cut the costs of creating jobs:* There are several reasons that hiring additional workers is so hard for small businesses. The tax system is too complicated. The payroll tax is too high. The capital gains tax is too high. Regulations and paperwork require-

ments are too burdensome and costly. We need to ease those burdens on small businesses.

REDUCING THE SIZE OF GOVERNMENT

The president's targeted tax plan won't ease that burden. Most small businesses can't afford the high-priced accountants who figure out complicated tax break formulas. The president proposes to give with the one hand, through tax incentives that few will use, while taking on the other, through tax and regulatory policies that hurt all small businesses. That is shortsighted and self-defeating. If we focus on cutting the cost of creating jobs, the country will be better off in the long run.

The president was also wrong in his March 1997 proposal. It will only increase the costs of government, resulting in either higher taxes or higher interest rates. We don't need more government. We need a smaller and smarter government that will increase opportunities in the private sector for all Americans, especially those Americans who want to get off welfare and have a chance to realize their dreams.

As the Congress and administration proceeds on a plan to put people to work, I hope we all keep these four principles in mind. The best thing that government can do is get out of the way and let the private sector get to work in putting people back to work and off welfare for good.

"Those who run job training
programs need to worry ... about
the encouragement and reassurance
they provide to help clients make the
transition into the labor market."

Job Training Programs Can Help
People Escape Poverty

Rebecca M. Blank

States can help their residents work their way out of poverty
through the establishment of effective job training programs, argues Rebecca M. Blank in the following viewpoint. Blank maintains that job training programs can succeed if the programs
counsel their clients about the realities of the job market, such
as low wages and angry bosses. In addition, she contends, successful programs will offer access to further training and provide public sector jobs. Blank is a social scientist and the author
of It Takes a Nation: A New Agenda for Fighting Poverty, from which this
viewpoint is taken.

As you read, consider the following questions:
1. What other kinds of assistance should be combined with
   employment programs, according to Blank?
2. According to the author, what was the employment rate for
   high school dropouts in 1994?
3. In Blank's view, what are the two contradictory demands of
   welfare reform?

There are many ways to run effective job training, and no one way is obviously "right." In fact, in different settings, with different populations, some very different models of job training have been effective. In short, it's not just what you do, but how you do it that makes a job program effective. Thus, rather than giving a detailed outline for employment programs, in this viewpoint I make recommendations about the design and operation of effective job programs that state and local program planners need to keep in mind as they revise and reform existing programs.

THE IMPORTANCE OF A GOOD STAFF

First, be clear that job search, employment, and training programs are different from cash assistance programs. States that operate employment programs as just another required mandate for their Aid to Families with Dependent Children (AFDC) clients are typically least successful in these programs. Such states run the job program out of the same office, with the same staff, and in much the same way as they run AFDC.

In contrast, programs that have been effective have typically dealt quite differently with their employment programs. They make sure their employment program is about jobs and staffed by people who understand that. This may mean hiring new staff or, at a minimum, retraining staff who were working with AFDC. Helping people find jobs is not the same as certifying them for cash assistance. . . .

Second, make sure the staff are enthusiastic about the program and promote the need and the opportunities for work with their clients. There's an element of excitement about good employment programs, communicated from the staff to the clients. It is an excitement about the possibilities of work, as well as about the opportunities this program will open to clients. People assigned to work programs are sometimes scared, sometimes reluctant, and almost always uncertain about what this work program will mean in their lives. Those who run job training programs need to worry not just about the details of program design, but also about the encouragement and reassurance they provide to help clients make the transition into the labor market.

Effective state job programs market themselves to their clients. At one particularly memorable job site, I was in a room where women were making phone calls to local employers asking about available jobs. The group was interrupted twice in an hour by an outside staff person who burst in, announcing he had just heard about a particular job that was open. He listed the necessary skills; was anyone interested? If not, he'd be back soon with another job. The message sent was that jobs *were* available and that the program was working with the women to try and locate them.

PROGRAMS SHOULD BE REALISTIC

Third, give clients realistic expectations about the jobs available to them. Many jobs will pay low wages; the boss may make constant and some-times unreasonable demands; there may be little slack for late-ness or misbehavior on the job; workers may be on their feet eight hours a day. Clients need to learn not only about the op-portunities, but also about the particular problems they are likely to face on their jobs.

One program in Chicago sets up mock situations and has clients act out their responses to an angry boss, an intimidating co-worker, or a rude customer. Another program explicitly counsels clients about both the advantages and the disadvantages of the jobs for which they are interviewing. When new workers have unrealistic expectations about the job they've located, they are less likely to stay in it. Finding a job and being fired in a few weeks may only make it harder to go out job hunting again.

In today's labor market, relatively few less-skilled clients in job programs are going to find initial jobs with good pay, pleas-ant working conditions, and interesting work. This is one reason why putting employment programs together with other forms of assistance—Earned Income Tax Credit (EITC) supplements, child support payments, health insurance, etc.—is so important. If job programs and job placements leave people worse off than before, with less income and all the demands of a crummy job, news of this will spread fast among clients. It will be all the harder to elicit interest and enthusiasm about finding a job and going to work.

DEVELOPING FOLLOW-UP PROGRAMS

Fourth, make sure job placement programs have a strong "follow-up" component, so that those who lose jobs can quickly return to job search and seek new employ-ment. Many people who have been out of the labor market will not be successful in their first job, or maybe even their second and third. Many current job programs operate on the assump-tion that once a job placement occurs, the program has been ef-fective and its work is over. Someone who is unemployed and without income three months later often reapplies for AFDC, and it might be months or years before she is again assigned to a work program.

The privately run Center for Employment Training (CET) vocational training program, which has been replicated around the country, is successful partly because its graduates are considered clients for life. Those who lose jobs can come back and be quickly reconnected with a network of employers and job options. The good news is that most programs find that clients need to come back only a few times before they connect with a job that works. Without the option to return and reaccess the resources of the employment system, however, some clients will too quickly be back in the same situation they started in.

PROGRAMS NEED MONEY AND SUPPORT

Training programs need to be designed and administered by financially stable organizations. Many community organizations that run training programs, instead, grapple with fluctuating funding and shifting political interest. . . .

Job training programs need a lot of money, and a lot of support to succeed. They need the commitment of both businesses for jobs and local schools for stability. They need to listen to the voices of participants to learn what's needed and devise an administrative structure that can change the program with the times.

Paul Osterman and Brenda A. Lautsch, *Dollars and Sense*, November/December 1996.

Fifth, realize that if many more women are required to enter employment programs—particularly long-term AFDC recipients—many of these women will require more than a few weeks of job search assistance before they are ready for employment. There is no cheap way to provide employment services to seriously disadvantaged populations, and to produce significant increases in earnings and employment. Many long-term public assistance recipients face multiple problems; some women are in abusive relationships, some are clinically depressed, some face substance abuse and addiction problems. Many of those who are long-term users of public assistance face some of these problems. These are not women who are going to be readily hired by employers. If we want *all* AFDC recipients to work, states must directly confront these problems in their job programs.

It may be cheaper to continue to provide cash assistance to some very disadvantaged women and children than to try and provide them with training and counseling that will help them move into steady employment. This is not to say that we shouldn't try to run job programs for these women, but merely that these programs will be more difficult and more expensive than most programs we are currently running for AFDC clients. Simply telling this group to "go out there and get a job" is unlikely to show many results. . . .

EXPAND TRAINING OPPORTUNITIES

Sixth, do not assume that training or education should precede job search. Particularly among people who have little labor market experience, there is increasing evidence that it is work experience that stimulates people to think about their lack of training and skills. Younger dropouts and women who have been out of the labor market for an extended period of time often lack the motivation to seriously participate in skill-building programs until they've been out working. Only with experience do they become motivated to go back into a classroom or into a vocational education program and improve their literacy or their math or acquire additional skills.

This is one reason why programs that simply provide job search assistance tend to be cost effective. They move people into work quickly, which is often the goal of someone who enters a job program. But ultimately, many less-skilled workers will need more skills before they will advance into higher-wage jobs. In some cases, workers will be able to get extra training with their employers. But in many cases, this is not possible.

If we are serious about trying to get people into better-paying jobs, then access to further training opportunities must be available to those who are motivated to take them. In many cases, this may not mean traditional classroom learning (although that is often a piece of any training program). Apprenticeship programs, vocational education programs, and on-the-job training programs may be far more effective for workers who are wary of returning to a school environment they left at an early age (often with bad memories of how they did in the classroom).

THE ROLE OF THE PUBLIC SECTOR

Seventh, plan to create some public sector jobs or subsidize some private sector jobs if your program wants to place a high share of the most disadvantaged population into the workforce. Among female high school dropouts, the unemployment rate was 16 percent in 1994; it was 14 percent among males. This means many less-skilled people who seek work will not immediately find jobs. If a large group of AFDC recipients were pushed into the labor market at once, the unemployment situation would only become worse, since the number of jobs available in the short term is typically not very expandable.

In addition, if states are trying to get the most disadvantaged population into work, some of them may simply not be employable in the private sector until they have work experience. For instance, we know that many employers are suspicious of workers who have not held a recent job or who have a criminal record, or they are very reluctant to hire younger black men from ghetto areas. A public assistance system that demands everyone be employed is closer to a command economy than a market economy; if everyone is to work, someone has to guarantee the "jobs of last resort" to those workers who are not hired by private employers. A six-month-long successful employment stint in a publicly created job can show an employer that this worker will show up on time and do the work assigned.

Public sector jobs create management problems. It is a major challenge to identify positions in public and nonprofit agencies, to match workers and slots, and to monitor both the worker's behavior and the employer's behavior so that the worker is provided with some attention and training. In short, this is neither a cheap nor an easy program to run, and it is not a program most states will want to run at a very large scale. On the other hand, public sector employment can provide an effective way to enforce work requirements regardless of the local rate of unemployment. . . .

An alternative to public sector job creation is short-term employer subsidies for hiring disadvantaged workers. Such programs create incentives for employers to provide jobs to workers they may not otherwise hire. On the one hand, employer subsidies avoid the management problems of running public sector job programs. On the other hand, they may be less effective at increasing employment, particularly if employers are wary about hiring workers who have been out of the mainstream labor market for long periods of time.

No Cheap Solutions

Eighth, expect that anything beyond basic job search assistance will not be cheap. The debate over welfare reform wants to hold onto two contradictory demands. First, we are demanding that people must find employment and cannot claim unlimited cash assistance. This has led states to run welfare-to-work programs. Second, we want to save money by cutting people off welfare. This will not happen if ending cash assistance means running more extensive work programs. In fact, the more that states focus on trying to move the most disadvantaged populations into employment, the more such work programs will cost and the smaller their short-term benefits will be, as they deal with clients who have very limited job skills.

There is no quick, easy, and cheap way to run a good job training program. Job search assistance—the least expensive type of job program—is often effective at increasing work but largely places people in very low-wage and unstable jobs which do not solve their ongoing economic problems. For these workers, ongoing child care supplements and earnings supplements will be necessary. Job training and education programs are much more expensive to run and provide much less immediate results but may increase long-run earnings opportunities. Clearly, a good state job program will provide both types of programs to different groups of people.

| "The ultimate goal of welfare reform is to promote marriage and family formation."

PROMOTING MARRIAGE WILL HELP THE POOR

William Tucker

Many people contend that the welfare system has helped create a culture of illegitimacy. In the following viewpoint, William Tucker argues that prior to its reform in 1996, the welfare system made it possible for unmarried women to support their children without the aid of a husband. According to Tucker, the values promoted by welfare were especially devastating to African-American families, which until the 1950s had adopted traditional Christian attitudes toward marriage and parenting. He asserts that for welfare reform to succeed, marriage and the formation of two-parent families must be encouraged. Tucker is the New York correspondent for the *American Spectator*, a conservative monthly periodical.

As you read, consider the following questions:

1. In the author's view, how will two-parent families help reduce teen pregnancy?
2. What are the three models of marriage in Africa, according to Tucker?
3. What are the European norms of family formation, according to the author?

W hen President Bill Clinton signed the welfare reform bill into law in August 1996, he instantaneously put an end to an entitlement that many on both sides of the political fence had long believed untouchable—the 60-year entitlement known as Aid to Families with Dependent Children (AFDC). The heart and soul of America's welfare program, AFDC had been costing the federal government more than $25 billion annually. In fact, it still will—instead of being carved up in Washington, however, that money will be distributed to the states in the form of block grants. Even so, the measure was the first significant welfare reform since the program began in 1936.

The extreme reactions from both sides showed just how emotionally charged the issue had become. Republicans proudly claimed the bill would end "the culture of dependency." Daniel Patrick Moynihan, on the other hand, predicted there would be "a million children thrown into the streets." Neither of these outcomes is terribly likely. Most of the money saved by the bill comes from cutting off benefits to illegal aliens, and it is more than likely that millions of current welfare mothers will simply find another state or federal program to subsidize them. Supplemental Security Income (SSI) Disability Benefits, now growing faster than AFDC ever did, is a prime candidate. The Earned Income Tax Credit program, which has become a vast, unpoliced subsidy to low-income people, is another.

THE RISE IN ILLEGITIMACY

Much more important for our national future is whether or not the moral implications of welfare reform take hold. Although few people discuss it openly, what welfare reform is really about is illegitimacy. The ultimate goal of welfare reform is to promote marriage and family formation. This is a cultural task—yet one in which our public policy has played a decisive, and disastrous, role.

Illegitimacy appears in all cultures. Given the facts of biology, it is always possible for an unmarried man and woman to conceive a child. Yet traditionally, the solution has been for the woman to marry, either the father of the child or a hastily arranged substitute. . . .

After AFDC became available in the 1950's and 1960's, this pattern was disrupted—for perhaps the first time in human history. Now a young woman could have one or two illegitimate children and then go on welfare. Census figures show that over the last thirty years, the number of children an unmarried woman bears in her lifetime has nearly tripled. Since she now had an independent means of support, her family lost control over her. She might even use welfare to escape her family. This support makes marriage unimportant. The single-parent family is born.

THE DESTRUCTION OF NORMS

This pattern in turn bred a species of men who have become irresponsible or indifferent to supporting women. They drift from woman to woman, having a baby here and a baby there. Soon things become so complicated that family formation is virtually impossible. The children of these unions, knowing nothing different, continue and exaggerate the pattern. Biology replaces culture.

To date, most of this cultural destruction has been limited to black America and remained entangled in racial politics and cultural guilt. Yet even this is about to change. As Charles Murray points out, the level of African-American illegitimacy is unlikely to rise much further simply because it has no place left to go. The significant changes will be in white illegitimacy. Norms are breaking down so fast that white unwed motherhood has already gone beyond the "tipping point" of 20 percent that first alerted Moynihan to the black problem in 1965.

David Blankenhorn, author of *Fatherless America,* reported being summoned to speak at an ordinary high school in Indiana where 30 percent of the graduating class was pregnant with illegitimate children. When he began counseling an auditorium full of students about the virtues of intact families he met a wall of animosity. Boys complained their fathers had never been around to help them. Girls solemnly proclaimed themselves capable of raising babies without men. Each of these declarations was met by thunderous applause from the assembled teenagers.

If nothing else, Blankenhorn's experience shows how, once the culture of illegitimacy gains a foothold, it is difficult to control. The hope is that the abolition of AFDC will lead people to perceive marriage as the solution to the single-parent family. People will start making long-term commitments and establishing a secure home before bringing children into the world. The state will no longer substitute as breadwinner. Millions of "missing men," many of them last sighted at Louis Farrakhan's Million Man March, will suddenly come home.

In the offing, crime will also be reduced because fathers will be at home disciplining their boys. Teenage pregnancy will abate because fathers will be there to protect their daughters from the amorous advances of young men, as well as offering them the emotional security to prevent them from throwing themselves at the first man who comes along. Parents would hand down their wisdom while providing a protective environment for their children. Still, the question remains: Will it work?

PREVIOUS RESPONSES TO PREGNANCY

There were, of course, major problems with family formation prior to the 1960's. Forgotten in the great abortion debate was the fact that many couples were forced into marriages by early pregnancies. Getting pregnant prior to 1960 almost always meant a couple quickly married. If the girl were too young, she would mysteriously disappear for a while into a home for wayward girls and her baby would be put up for adoption. Going on welfare was generally not a respectable option.

Studies of working class neighborhoods have shown that, prior to 1970, as many as half the marriages took place under these circumstances. Often pregnancy was simply a way of sealing a bond that already existed. A couple might sleep together or even live together until they "made a mistake" and got pregnant, at which point they would marry. More rarely, a woman might trap a man into marriage by deliberately becoming pregnant, or even feigning pregnancy.

The great irony is that when birth control and abortion came along in the 1960's, both were touted by liberal advocates as tools for strengthening marriage by avoiding these hasty and premature unions. As far back as the 1920's, Bertrand Russell argued for "trial marriages" on the grounds that they would help people make better choices. This idea was actually institutionalized after the 1960's by the widely adopted practice of "living together."

Yet at that very moment of sexual liberation, Americans discovered that, given enough freedom in such matters, people might not marry at all. Without the Damoclean sword of the shotgun marriage, men seem much less willing to make marriage commitments. Given the freedom not to have babies, women at times seemed content to have them without marrying men. Neither did the practice of living together pan out. Studies have shown that couples who live together before marriage are actually less committed to each other and more likely to divorce.

THE LINK BETWEEN GOVERNMENT AND ILLEGITIMACY

Arriving hand in hand with the age of illegitimacy was the age of big government. In fact, the two seem inextricable. In Sweden, where 70 percent of GNP is now controlled by the government, permanent unions are fast disappearing. Illegitimacy rates are approaching 60 percent and "living together" in shifting and uncommitted relationships has almost replaced marriage altogether. Worst of all, the welfare state has spawned its most virulent organism, the aggressive bureaucrat who actively intervenes in domestic situations and encourages family break-up.

Yet even if we beat back the welfare state, we are still left with the thorny question of what to do in a situation where marriage and family formation have virtually vanished as social institutions. It is no exaggeration to say that among the American underclass there are very few surviving customs that lead people into stable marital unions. Expecting happy marriages to spring out of the soil by abolishing welfare is like expecting a Western economy to spring up in Russia with the collapse of Communism. The potential is there but there are many habits to be relearned.

Perhaps the best place to start is to realize that, historically and anthropologically, marriage among people of African descent simply has not been the same institution as among people of European and Oriental descent. The traditional explanation of the historical weakness of the American black family, which led to its virtual dissolution under the welfare system, has been the experience of slavery. The black family, according to this interpretation, was fatally weakened by centuries of servitude. Families were sold apart, children torn from their mothers and fathers, women raped and forced to bear the children of their masters. Family traditions were lost forever.

MARRIAGE IN AFRICA

There is a great deal of truth in this explanation, but it is not the whole truth. Even a cursory look at the anthropology of the situation reveals that marriage in Africa is an entirely different institution than marriage in most other parts of the world. (Most anthropologists know this but are reluctant to say it out loud for fear of being the bearers of uncomfortable truths.)

West Africa—the home of most Africans who came to America—has long been known to anthropologists as the world's "matrilineal belt." In Europe and Asia, nearly all cultures practice "dual descent," meaning that ancestry is traced through both the maternal and paternal lines. But in West Africa, descent is traced only through the maternal line. Children belong to their mothers and often take their names. Men have very weak paternal claims. . . .

A man can take several wives, mainly because he does not have to do much to support them. Women generally provide at least half the sustenance for themselves and their children. A man will build a hut for each of his co-wives and provide land for them to farm, but his relation with his children remains somewhat distant. Such marriages are extremely weak and vulnerable. Since children belong to their mothers, women can take them and return to their natal families any time they want.

Marriage Lowers Poverty Rates

According to data released by the U.S. Census Bureau . . . black Americans should look at marriage more seriously. While about one-third of black Americans live under the poverty level, statistics reveal that only 9 percent of black married couples live at that level (only 3 percent of white married couples live in poverty). . . .

Nearly 75 percent of American children living in fatherless households will experience poverty before the age of 11. Only 20 percent of those raised by two parents will be impoverished.

Joseph H. Brown, *Headway*, September 1997.

Over the past several centuries, tribal practices have gradually been superseded by Christianity and Islam. Christianity preaches monogamy while Islam allows polygamy, but both emphasize that a man should be the principal support of his family. As a result, both are considered modernizing influences. These three models for marriage—Christian monogamy, Moslem polygamy, and tribal polygamy—are still very much in contention in Africa today.

In light of this history, the story of the people of African descent who came to America takes on a much different hue. Slavery indeed tore apart families in individual instances and denied Africans their freedom. But it also Christianized Africans and converted them to Western monogamy. Polygamy was outlawed very early by slaveowners—mainly as a moral offense—and monogamy was encouraged. As a result, American blacks have a history that is at least as much Western as it is African. . . .

By adopting Christianity, African-Americans became culturally indistinguishable from everyone else. As Herbert Gutman documented in his monumental study, *The Black Family in Slavery and Freedom, 1750–1920*, the vast majority of African-Americans established marriages and were raising children in two-parent homes during slavery. After the Civil War, in one Virginia County, 60 percent of the adult black women registered marriages in one year—1866—when concerns arose that these slave marriages would not be recognized as legal. This pattern continued well into the twentieth century. Studies of American blacks through the 1940's show they were living in two-parent homes that were hardly distinguishable from other ethnic groups.

WELFARE DESTROYS FAMILY FORMATION

However, there were cultural weaknesses. Most prominent was the custom—common in matrilineal cultures—of allowing a young girl to have one or two early illegitimacies *before* she married. In fact, if you examine carefully the primary sources that Gutman uses to prove his thesis, you find it graphically illustrated.

Gutman's most telling documents are the careful accounts of births and marriages kept on three major plantations in North Carolina and Louisiana over nearly a hundred years. As Gutman points out, the records show that 80 percent of slave children were being raised in two-parent homes. But they also show something else: These children were not always born to the same mother and father. The most common pattern was for a woman to have one or two children out of wedlock (usually to a "father unknown") and then settle into a permanent union with one man. Thus, the paradoxical result—while almost 40 percent of the children born on these plantations were technically illegitimate, fully 80 percent ended up living in two-parent homes with both a mother and father present.

This is why Aid to Families with Dependent Children has had such a devastating impact on black family formation. AFDC was shaped around middle-class norms. Originally conceived as a small stipend for widows and orphans, it was eventually extended to divorced women and ultimately women who had never married. The assumption was that these groups were small, self-limiting, and not likely to grow.

What the policymakers who made these decisions did not understand was that there are vast cultural differences between African and European/Asian family formation. Using European norms, these policymakers assumed a model where people get married, have children, and then occasionally, through choice or calamity, become single parents. At this point, AFDC would step in and help out. Even today, liberals persist in talking about welfare as a program that "helps people who are down on their luck" get "back on their feet again."

What welfare did instead was to disrupt the process of family formation, particularly among blacks. Whereas an African-American woman once had one or two illegitimacies and then married, she now has one or two illegitimacies and then goes on welfare. Thus the creation of a single-parent culture with AFDC as its sole economic underpinning.

TWO-PARENT FAMILIES ARE THE SOLUTION

The principal goal of welfare reform, then, is not to turn the single-mother home into a viable economic unit. This is virtually impossible and hardly desirable as well. What we can hope is that, given a more natural constellation of forces—and with a lot of cultural encouragement—underclass men and women will start forming families again.

| "In spite of the economic costs of teen pregnancy, . . . attacks on and censorship of sex education programs are increasing."

SEX EDUCATION CAN HELP END THE CYCLE OF POVERTY

Mary Loftin Grimes

In the following viewpoint, Mary Loftin Grimes argues that comprehensive sex education is among the reforms needed to end the cycle of poor teenagers having children. She also maintains that teenagers who have become parents should have access to child care, job training, and other programs that will keep them off welfare. The United States should not be a nation that traps children and young parents in poverty, Grimes asserts. Grimes is a professor of education at the University of North Florida in Jacksonville.

As you read, consider the following questions:

1. What proportion of nonwhite live births in the author's state were to females between the ages of ten and fourteen?
2. What social conditions do liberal advocates believe cause early pregnancy, according to Grimes?
3. According to the author, what is the contemporary equivalent to Jonathan Swift's 1723 proposal?

After many months of debate in the courts and the press, my local school board has established its right to incorporate sex education into the curriculum. Currently that decision remains on hold, as debate continues about curricular scope and sequence. Those advocating inclusion of information to help children protect themselves against unplanned pregnancy and sexually transmitted diseases appear to have prevailed. Still unresolved is the issue of when to introduce this information, with some proponents arguing for early intervention at sixth or seventh grade level, while others favor deferral of such information to the senior high years.

WORRISOME PREGNANCY STATISTICS

This debate has become more than an academic issue for me. My teaching assignment in spring 1995 included supervision of interns at an inner-city high school, where for many young students education has obviously not had the desired effect of preventing pregnancy. One teacher, a former Army medic, carries a cellular telephone to be available for medical emergencies such as onset of labor.

The statistics are not reassuring for this group: locally 10 percent of all live births occurred to mothers who were eighteen or younger in 1994. Most of these mothers were unwed. This group accounted for disproportionate numbers of low (5.5 pounds or less) and very low birth-weight (two pounds or less) babies, as well as a high incidence of infant mortality. They also manifested significant health risks before delivery, with anemia and other complications associated with inadequate prenatal care occurring regularly among their numbers. At the state level, 5.5 of every 1,000 non-white live births were to females aged ten to fourteen. And while the Sex Information and Education Council of the United States (SIECUS) reports a decline in births to very young teenagers in 1994, the United States continues to have higher rates of teen pregnancy and childbearing than do thirty-six other developed countries. According to the *Journal of the American Medical Association*, American teens are far more likely to get pregnant than European teens and less likely to seek abortions once they are.

One may assume that few ten-year-old females enter into the state of motherhood deliberately. Their levels of ignorance about conception and contraception are well documented in anecdotal accounts. Years ago some of my female secondary students accepted the myth, perpetrated by their boyfriends, no doubt, that engaging in sexual intercourse would improve their complexions. (Never mind what it did for their figures!) And while re-searchers have not found education to affect the incidence of sexual activity, they do note an increase in responsible behaviors where early and sustained sex education is provided.

The Relationship Between Pregnancy and Poverty

So I am concerned that reproductive and contraceptive informa-tion will get to local students—if indeed it ever progresses be-yond the planning stage—too late to reverse the trend toward parenthood at younger and younger ages, to mothers increas-ingly incapable of providing for their offspring. And yet it ap-pears that those same groups who fought so hard to keep sex education out of our schools are now crusading to withdraw support for basic needs to mothers and children caught in the double binds of ignorance and poverty. In spite of the high inci-dence of pregnancy and sexually transmitted diseases among teens who received no sex education, and in spite of the eco-nomic costs of teen pregnancy, including the personal conse-quences of becoming a school dropout with its attendent increased likelihood of poverty and welfare dependency, wide-spread opposition still exists in this country to prevention pro-grams such as condom distribution in the schools. Rather, attacks on and censorship of sex education programs are in-creasing. The religious right's assumption that sex education causes pregnancy posits avoidance as the solution to the prob-lem and accuses welfare programs of feeding the problem, im-plying thereby that the sexual behaviors of the underprivileged are dictated by innate depravity.

More liberal advocates see poverty as the root cause, with protection and prevention as appropriate responses. They note a correlation between teen pregnancy and a wide range of educa-tional deficits, including untreated learning problems, low educational aspirations, and the pregnant teen's mother's educa-tional attainment level. They also find a range of social condi-tions related to early pregnancy, such as abusive households, single parenthood, and weak family value structures. Character-istic of both males and females who become teen parents is low self-esteem.

Faced with the magnitude and complexity of this issue, it is not surprising that we are divided over a solution. [Former British prime minister] John Major's solution—"We should condemn more and understand less"—seems to have been em-braced by those in power. The assumption that if one has a big enough whip one can accomplish miracles appears to undergird

proposals for welfare reform. These proposals appear further in-
fused with the Calvinist assumption that the poor and oppressed
are going to do wrong, and the only way to inhibit sinful behavior is to punish them.

BREAKING THE CYCLE OF POVERTY

Whether the problem of unwanted and unsupported offspring
will diminish when federal assistance is denied those who own
the problem remains to be seen. Clearly, moral instruction alone
is an inadequate deterrent, yet many state sex education programs continue to omit information on abortion, contraception,
and avoidance of sexually transmitted diseases. Conservatives appear unwilling to support child care, job training, and other assistance programs necessary for young mothers to remove
themselves from the welfare rolls. Yet they propose no transitional plan to address the needs of millions of infants and children trapped in poverty through no error other than that of having been born.

A FULL-SCALE ATTACK ON TEENAGE PREGNANCIES

We must drastically reduce the number of high-risk children requiring extra care, and that means successfully attacking the epidemic of teenage pregnancies. To stop the cycle of poverty leading to hopelessness, poor education, poor health, joblessness,
welfare dependency, crime, prison, developmental disabilities,
schools that do not work and cannot work, and taxes (which are
resented because the programs they support do not cure the
problems), we have to invest much more in every child born at
high risk than we do now, and at the same time we should aim
to cut teenage pregnancies by 90 percent. Realistically, a lesser
goal will not enable us to reach all children who need help. To
achieve such a dramatic reduction in teen pregnancies requires
courage and leadership.

Irving B. Harris, *Children in Jeopardy: Can We Break the Cycle of Poverty?*, 1996.

If they are to break the cycle of children having children,
America's young people need options other than poverty and despair. Great Britain has mandated sex education in state schools,
in response to the growing problem of teen childbearing. Teachers there are free to dispense contraceptive information, upon re-
quest. Several promising initiatives are underway in our country
as well, although most of these address child rearing rather than
contraception. In 1992, Baltimore initiated a contraceptive implant program for high-risk youth, thereby delaying fertility for

participants. Kentucky has the Teen Age Troubadours, who explain to their peers the consequences of risky behavior. Baby Think It Over, a doll that cries until a key attached to its "parent's" wrist is held in its back for twenty minutes, is designed to include males in pregnancy prevention programs by allowing them to experience some of the realities of unplanned parenthood. The Nike Footed Health Workers provide first-time teen mothers with assistance and training. Locally, a Young Parents' Center provides support, including on-site child care, to approximately 500 school-age mothers each year (half the number who become pregnant), so that they may continue their education. And the 1995 Florida Legislature proposed funding for an additional 20,000 day care slots for low-income children, thereby extending some additional relief to teen parents.

However strongly one feels about the issue, it seems unrealistic to expect today's teens to practice abstinence for a decade after their sexual maturity. Policies that improve educational and earning opportunities contribute directly and indirectly to reducing teen pregnancy and childbearing. The components of an effective reform program to help lessen the incidence of teen pregnancy include sex education, job training, health care, and child care. Most of these issues were addressed in President Bill Clinton's Work and Responsibility Act (June 1994). If this country is to meet its obligation to provide a decent standard of living for all infants and children, all public institutions—schools, community health, mental health, and social service agencies—must work together to solve the problem of teen pregnancy. The consequences of not doing so are grave. [Clinton's proposal was superseded by Congress's 1996 welfare reform bill. That bill restricts teenage parents' ability to receive welfare, provides $13.9 billion for child care through 2002, and includes $75 million for abstinence education.]

Do Not Destroy Children's Futures

In 1723 Jonathan Swift proposed that the English solve the Irish population problem by using unwanted babies as sources of food and fine leather. The contemporary metaphorical equivalent of Swift's proposal is "Just Say No" to programs for children—starve them, and exacerbate class divisions in the process. The sane alternative to that course is to intervene with accurate and complete information early and often; to provide counseling and assistance; to recognize that in spite of our wisdom and advice, many young people are going to be sexually active; to prepare young people to be responsible for the consequences of their sexual behaviors, both to avoid unwanted pregnancies and to preserve their health; and to provide those who have become parents and wish to better their economic prospects with job training, child care, transportation assistance, and other services required for this group to succeed. Do not let us become a nation that eats babies.

PERIODICAL BIBLIOGRAPHY

The following articles have been selected to supplement the diverse views presented in this chapter. Addresses are provided for periodicals not indexed in the *Readers' Guide to Periodical Literature*, the *Alternative Press Index*, the *Social Sciences Index*, or the *Index to Legal Periodicals and Books*.

Virginia D. Abernethy	"To Reform Welfare, Reform Immigration," *St. Croix Review*, April 1997. Available from PO Box 244, Stillwater, MN 55082.
Skip Barry	"Today's Housing Crisis," *Z Magazine*, February 1997.
David Caprara	"'Moral Fiber' Will Fix Holes in Welfare," *Insight*, March 14, 1994. Available from PO Box 91022, Washington, DC 20090-1022.
Stephanie Coontz and Donna Franklin	"When the Marriage Penalty Is Marriage," *New York Times*, October 28, 1997.
Jason DeParle	"Cutting Welfare Rolls but Raising Questions," *New York Times*, May 7, 1997.
Jason DeParle	"Learning Poverty Firsthand," *New York Times Magazine*, April 27, 1997.
Peter Edelman	"The Worst Thing Bill Clinton Has Done," *Atlantic Monthly*, March 1997.
Stan Guthrie	"Learning to Care," *Moody*, October 1994. Available from the Moody Bible Institute, 820 N. LaSalle Blvd., Chicago, IL 60610.
Robert Krol and Shirley Svorny	"Inner Cities and Long-Run Government Policy," *Jobs & Capital*, Spring 1994. Available from MIJCF, 1250 Fourth St., 2nd Fl., Santa Monica, CA 90401-1353.
Lawrence M. Mead	"Conflicting Worlds of Welfare Reform," *First Things*, August/September 1997.
William Murchison	"Time to End the Welfare State?" *Conservative Chronicle*, February 12, 1997. Available from PO Box 11297, Des Moines, IA 50340-1297.
Elena Neuman	"A New Lease on Life Beyond the Inner City," *Insight*, March 14, 1994.
Ellen Pader	"Redefining the Home," *New York Times*, May 7, 1997.
E.C. Pasour Jr.	"The Government as Robin Hood," *Freeman*, December 1994. Available from the Foundation for Economic Education, 30 S. Broadway, Irvington-on-Hudson, NY 10533.
Mark J. Stern	"What We Talk About When We Talk About Welfare," *Tikkun*, November/December 1994.

FOR FURTHER DISCUSSION

CHAPTER 1

1. Bob Herbert argues that welfare programs have kept millions of children out of poverty. Dick Armey contends that children who live in families that receive welfare are more likely than other children to become welfare recipients when they reach adulthood. After reading these viewpoints, do you think it is more important to focus on the present conditions of poor children or what their lives will be like when they become adults? Explain your decision.

2. The extent of economic inequality is disputed by the *National Catholic Reporter* and John C. Weicher. After reading their viewpoints, do you think that economic inequality is a relevant yardstick when measuring the severity of poverty? Why or why not? Should poverty be based on a relative measurement— how much money one has compared to other people—or an absolute measurement? Explain your answer.

3. Bradley Schiller's central thesis is that the "working poor" problem is less extensive than the Census numbers suggest. He uses a variety of statistics to support his argument. Which statistics, if any, do you think best support his argument? Explain your answer.

CHAPTER 2

1. The relationship between single mothers and poverty is explored in the viewpoints by Andrea Sheldon and Mimi Abramovitz. Sheldon focuses on the moral behavior of these women, while Abramovitz contends that market forces lead to their poverty. Which author do you think offers a more accurate depiction of the lives of these women? Explain your answer.

2. Robert Lieberman refers to books written by George Orwell in the 1930s to bolster his argument that society needs to offer the poor more economic opportunities. Do you think the connections he draws between the societies Orwell describes and modern-day America are valid? Why or why not?

3. Writing for a socialist periodical, Linda Featheringill concludes that capitalism is the cause of poverty. George Gilder's viewpoint, which first appeared in the *Wall Street Journal*, asserts that the welfare state is to blame. Does knowing the source of these viewpoints affect how you view the authors' conclusions? If the sources were switched, would your opinion of these viewpoints be affected? Explain your answers.

CHAPTER 3

1. Alec R. Levenson, Elaine Reardon, and Stefanie R. Schmidt cite statistics on the low educational achievement of many welfare recipients; they conclude that such people will have difficulty finding a job that will keep them out of poverty. Kenneth Weinstein uses a series of anecdotes to show how hard work can lead to wealth, even for people who lack a college education. Do you think that the typical welfare recipient, as described by Levenson, Reardon, and Schmidt, could achieve successes similar to the people described by Weinstein? Defend your answer. What approach do you think could best help poor people to achieve success? Would education or job opportunities be more effective? Why?

2. After reading the viewpoints by John McDermott and Mark Wilson, do you think that raising the minimum wage is an effective way to reduce poverty? If so, explain what you think a fair minimum wage would be. If not, which of Wilson's suggestions do you think would benefit workers the most?

CHAPTER 4

1. In her viewpoint, Ruth Sidel argues that the American government should adopt family policies similar to those found in Western Europe. Michael Tanner asserts that existing government welfare programs are already bogged down in bureaucracy. After reading these selections, do you think that a universal family policy would be practical? Why or why not? Does the size of the United States relative to the size of European nations affect your decision? Explain.

2. Howard Husock argues that overly stringent building codes have helped cause the housing shortage. He contends that relaxing these codes would make it easier to build low-cost housing, such as single-room-occupancy hotels (SROs), that poor people could afford. Do you think that building codes should be altered to allow for the construction of low-cost housing? Is it acceptable for poor people to live in housing that does not meet existing regulations? Explain your answers.

3. This chapter offers a variety of approaches to helping poor people. Which alternatives do you think would be most effective? Are there other methods that you would suggest? Defend your answers with references to the viewpoints.

ORGANIZATIONS TO CONTACT

The editors have compiled the following list of organizations concerned with the issues debated in this book. The descriptions are derived from materials provided by the organizations. All have publications or information available for interested readers. The list was compiled on the date of publication of the present volume; the information provided here may change. Be aware that many organizations take several weeks or longer to respond to inquiries, so allow as much time as possible.

The Brookings Institution
1775 Massachusetts Ave. NW, Washington, DC 20036-2188
(202) 797-6000 • fax: (202) 797-6004
e-mail: brookinfo@brook.edu • web address: www.brookings.edu

The institution is devoted to nonpartisan research, education, and publication in economics, government, foreign policy, and the social sciences. Its principal purposes are to aid in the development of sound public policies and to promote public understanding of issues of national importance. It publishes the quarterly journal the *Brookings Review*, which periodically includes articles on poverty, and numerous books, including *The Urban Underclass*.

Cato Institute
1000 Massachusetts Ave. NW, Washington, DC 20001-5403
(202) 842-0200 • fax: (202) 842-3490
e-mail: cato@cato.org • web address: www.cato.org

The institute is a libertarian public policy research organization that advocates limited government. It has published a variety of literature concerning poverty in its quarterly *Cato Journal* and in its Policy Analysis series.

Center of Concern
3700 13th St. NE, Washington, DC 20017
(202) 635-2757 • fax: (202) 832-9494
e-mail: coc@igc.apc.org • web address: www.coc.org/coc/

Center of Concern engages in social analysis, theological reflection, policy advocacy, and public education on issues of justice and peace. Its programs and writings include subjects such as international development, women's roles, economic alternatives, and a theology based on justice for all peoples. It publishes the bimonthly newsletter *Center Focus* as well as numerous papers and books, including *Opting for the Poor: A Challenge for North Americans*.

Center on Budget and Policy Priorities
820 First St. NE, Suite 510, Washington, DC 20002
(202) 408-1080 • fax: (202) 408-1056
e-mail: center@center.cbpp.org • web address: www.cbpp.org

The center promotes better public understanding of the impact of federal and state governmental spending policies and programs primarily affecting low- and moderate-income Americans. It acts as a research center and information clearinghouse for the media, national and local organizations, and individuals. The center publishes numerous fact sheets, articles, and reports, including *The Safety Net Delivers: The Effects of Government Benefit Programs in Reducing Poverty*.

Children's Defense Fund (CDF)
25 E St. NW, Washington, DC 20001
(202) 628-8787
e-mail: cdfinfo@childrensdefense.org
web address: www.childrensdefense.org

CDF works to promote the interests of children in America. It pays particular attention to the needs of poor, minority, and disabled children. Its publications include *The State of America's Children 1998* and *Wasting America's Future: The Children's Defense Fund's Report on the Costs of Child Poverty*.

Coalition on Human Needs
1000 Wisconsin Ave. NW, Washington, DC 20007
(202) 342-0726 • fax: (202) 338-1856
e-mail: chn@chn.org

The coalition is a federal advocacy organization that works in such areas as federal budget and tax policy, housing, education, health care, and public assistance. It lobbies for adequate federal funding for welfare, Medicaid, and other social services. Its publications include *How the Poor Would Remedy Poverty*, the *Directory of National Human Needs Organizations*, and the biweekly legislative newsletter the *Human Needs Report*.

Economic Policy Institute
1660 L St. NW, Suite 1200, Washington, DC 20036
(202) 775-8810 • (800) 374-4844 (publications) • (202) 331-5510
(Washington, DC)
e-mail: blustig@epinet.org • web address: www.epinet.org

The institute was established in 1986 to pursue research and public education to help define a new economic strategy for the United States. Its goal is to identify policies that can provide prosperous, fair, and balanced economic growth. It publishes numerous policy studies, briefing papers, and books, including the titles *State of Working America* and *Declining American Incomes and Living Standards*.

The Heritage Foundation
214 Massachusetts Ave. NE, Washington, DC 20002-4999
(202) 546-4400 • fax: (202) 546-8328
e-mail: info@heritage.org • web address: www.heritage.org

The foundation is a public policy research institute dedicated to the principles of free competitive enterprise, limited government, individual liberty, and a strong national defense. The foundation publishes the monthly newsletter *Insider* and *Heritage Today*, a newsletter published six times per year, as well as various reports and journals.

Institute for Food and Development Policy

398 60th St., Oakland, CA 94618
(510) 654-4400 • fax: (510) 654-4551
e-mail: foodfirst@igc.apc.org • web address: www.foodfirst.org

The institute is a research, documentation, and public education center focusing on the social and economic causes of world hunger. It believes that there is enough food in the world to adequately feed everyone, but hunger results "when people lack control over the resources they need to produce food." It publishes the quarterly *Food First Backgrounders* as well as numerous articles, pamphlets, and books, including *An Update of World Hunger: Twelve Myths.*

National Alliance to End Homelessness

1518 K St. NW, Suite 206, Washington, DC 20005
(202) 638-1526 • fax: (202) 638-4664
e-mail: naeh@naeh.org • web address: www.naeh.org

The alliance is a national organization committed to the ideal that no American should have to be homeless. It works to secure more effective national and local policies to aid the homeless. Its publications include *What You Can Do to Help the Homeless* and the monthly newsletter *Alliance.*

National Council of La Raza (NCLR)

1111 19th St. NW, Suite 1000, Washington, DC 20036
(202) 785-1670 • fax: (202) 785-0851

NCLR is a national organization that promotes civil rights and economic opportunities for Hispanics. It provides technical assistance to Hispanic organizations engaged in community development, including economic development, housing, employment and training, business assistance, health, and other fields. NCLR publishes a quarterly newsletter, *Agenda*, as well as other issue-specific newsletters on poverty.

National Student Campaign Against Hunger and Homelessness (NSCAHH)

11965 Venice Blvd., Suite 408, Los Angeles, CA 90066
(800) 664-8647 • (310) 397-5270 ext. 323 • fax: (310) 391-0053
e-mail: nscah@aol.com • web address: www.pirg.org/nscahh/

NSCAHH is a network of college and high school students, educators, and community leaders who work to fight hunger and homelessness in the United States and around the world. Its mission is to create a generation of student/community activists who will explore and understand the root causes of poverty and who will initiate positive change through service and action. It publishes the quarterly newsletter *Students Making a Difference* as well as numerous manuals, fact sheets, and handbooks.

Population Reference Bureau, Inc. (PRB)
1875 Connecticut Ave. NW, Suite 520, Washington, DC 20009-5728
(202) 483-1100 • fax: (202) 328-3937
e-mail: popref@prb.org • web address: www.prb.org/prb/
PRB gathers, interprets, and disseminates information on national and world population trends. Its publications include the quarterly *Population Bulletin* and the monthly *Population Today*.

Poverty and Race Research Action Council (PRRAC)
1711 Connecticut Ave. NW, # 207, Washington, DC 20009
(202) 387-9887 • fax: (202) 387-0764
e-mail: prrac@aol.com
PRRAC was established by civil rights, antipoverty, and legal services groups. It works to develop antiracism and antipoverty strategies and provides funding for research projects that support advocacy work. It publishes the bimonthly newsletter *Poverty & Race*.

Progressive Policy Institute (PPI)
316 Pennsylvania Ave. SE, Suite 555, Washington, DC 20003
(202) 547-0001
e-mail: webmaster@dlcppi.org
PPI develops policy alternatives to the conventional liberal-conservative political debate. It advocates social policies that move beyond merely maintaining the poor to liberating them from poverty and dependency. Its publications include *Microenterprise: Human Reconstruction in America's Inner Cities* and *Social Service Vouchers: Bringing Choice and Competition to Social Services*.

BIBLIOGRAPHY OF BOOKS

Mimi Abramovitz — *Regulating the Lives of Women: Social Welfare Policy from Colonial Times to the Present.* Rev. ed. Boston: South End Press, 1996.

Mimi Abramovitz — *Under Attack, Fighting Back: Women and Welfare in the United States.* New York: Monthly Review Press, 1996.

Randy Albelda and Chris Tilly — *Glass Ceilings and Bottomless Pits.* Boston: South End Press, 1997.

Rebecca M. Blank — *It Takes a Nation: A New Agenda for Fighting Poverty.* New York: Russell Sage Foundation, 1997.

David Bornstein — *The Price of a Dream.* Chicago: University of Chicago Press, 1997.

David Card and Alan B. Krueger — *Myth and Measurement: The New Economics of the Minimum Wage.* Princeton, NJ: Princeton University Press, 1995.

Sheila Collins — *Let Them Eat Ketchup! The Politics of Poverty and Inequality.* New York: Monthly Review Press, 1996.

Alex Counts — *Give Us Credit.* New York: Times Books, 1996.

Sheldon Danziger and Peter Gottschalk — *America Unequal.* Cambridge, MA: Harvard University Press, 1995.

Leon Dash — *Rosa Lee: A Mother and Her Family in Urban America.* New York: BasicBooks, 1996.

Kathryn Edin and Laura Lein — *Making Ends Meet: How Single Mothers Survive Welfare and Low-Wage Work.* New York: Russell Sage Foundation, 1997.

Herbert J. Gans — *The War Against the Poor: The Underclass and Anti-Poverty Policy.* New York: BasicBooks, 1995.

Robert Halpern — *Rebuilding the Inner City: A History of Neighborhood Initiatives to Address Poverty in the United States.* New York: Columbia University Press, 1995.

Irving B. Harris — *Children in Jeopardy: Can We Break the Cycle of Poverty?* New Haven, CT: Yale Child Study Center, 1996.

Chester Hartman, ed. — *Double Exposure: Poverty & Race in America.* Armonk, NY: M.E. Sharpe, 1996.

Desmond King — *The Politics of Unemployment and Welfare Policy in the United States and Great Britain.* Chicago: University of Chicago Press, 1995.

Lawrence M. Mead — *The New Paternalism: Supervisory Approaches to Poverty.* Washington, DC: Brookings Institution, 1997.

Peter Medoff and Holly Sklar	*Streets of Hope: The Fall and Rise of an Urban Neighborhood.* Boston: South End Press, 1994.
John H. Miller, ed.	*Curing World Poverty: The New Role of Property.* St. Louis: Social Justice Review, 1994.
Daniel Patrick Moynihan	*Miles to Go: A Personal History of Social Policy.* Cambridge, MA: Harvard University Press, 1996.
Margery G. Nichelason	*Homeless or Hopeless?* Minneapolis: Lerner Publications, 1994.
Demetra Smith Nightingale and Robert H. Haveman	*The Work Alternative: Welfare Reform and the Realities of the Job Market.* Washington, DC: Urban Institute, 1995.
Ralph de Costa Nunez	*The New Poverty: Homeless Families in America.* New York: Insight Books, 1996.
James T. Patterson	*America's Struggle Against Poverty, 1900–1994.* Cambridge, MA: Harvard University Press, 1995.
Robert Rector and William F. Lauber	*America's Failed $5.4 Trillion War on Poverty.* Washington, DC: Heritage Foundation, 1995.
D. Eric Schansberg	*Poor Policy: How Government Harms the Poor.* Boulder, CO: Westview Press, 1996.
Hans F. Sennholz	*Up from Poverty: Reflections on the Ills of Public Assistance.* Irvington-on-Hudson, NY: Foundation for Economic Education, 1997.
Arloc Sherman	*Wasting America's Future: The Children's Defense Fund's Report on the Costs of Child Poverty.* Boston: Beacon Press, 1994.
Ruth Sidel	*Keeping Women and Children Last: America's War on the Poor.* New York: Penguin, 1996.
David Simon and Edward Burns	*The Corner: A Year in the Life of an Inner-City Neighborhood.* New York: Broadway Books, 1997.
Holly Sklar	*Chaos or Community?: Seeking Solutions, Not Scapegoats, for Bad Economics.* Boston: South End Press, 1995.
Michael Tanner	*The End of Welfare: Fighting Poverty in the Civil Society.* Washington, DC: Cato Institute, 1996.
Dorothy Van Soest	*The Global Crisis of Violence: Common Problems, Universal Causes, Shared Solutions.* Washington, DC: National Association of Social Workers, 1997.
John C. Weicher	*Federal Housing Policy: Programs, Problems, and Solutions.* Washington, DC: Brookings Institution, 1997.
William Julius Wilson	*When Work Disappears: The World of the New Urban Poor.* New York: Knopf, 1996.
David Zucchino	*Myth of the Welfare Queen.* New York: Scribner, 1997.

INDEX